# SAFE
# ALL
# ALONG

# SAFE
# ALL
# ALONG

Trading Our Fears and Anxieties
for God's Unshakable Peace

## Katie Davis Majors

MULTNOMAH

All Scripture quotations, unless otherwise indicated, are taken from the Holy Bible, New International Version®, NIV®. Copyright © 1973, 1978, 1984, 2011 by Biblica, Inc.™ Used by permission of Zondervan. All rights reserved worldwide. (www.zondervan.com). The "NIV" and "New International Version" are trademarks registered in the United States Patent and Trademark Office by Biblica Inc.™ Scripture quotations marked (ESV) are taken from the ESV® Bible (The Holy Bible, English Standard Version®), copyright © 2001 by Crossway, a publishing ministry of Good News Publishers. Used by permission. All rights reserved. Scripture quotations marked (NKJV) are taken from the New King James Version®. Copyright © 1982 by Thomas Nelson. Used by permission. All rights reserved. Scripture quotations marked (NLT) are taken from the Holy Bible, New Living Translation, copyright © 1996, 2004, 2015 by Tyndale House Foundation. Used by permission of Tyndale House Publishers, Carol Stream, Illinois 60188. All rights reserved.

Italics in Scripture quotations reflect the author's added emphasis.

Published in the United States by Multnomah, an imprint of Random House,
a division of Penguin Random House LLC.

MULTNOMAH® and its mountain colophon are registered trademarks
of Penguin Random House LLC.

Published in association with Yates & Yates, www.yates2.com.

Hardback ISBN 978-0-593-44511-2
Ebook ISBN 978-0-593-44512-9

The Library of Congress catalog record is available at https://lccn.loc.gov/2022042445.

Printed in Canada on acid-free paper.

waterbrookmultnomah.com

9 8 7 6 5 4 3 2

Book design by Jo Anne Metsch

SPECIAL SALES Most Multnomah books are available at special quantity discounts when purchased in bulk by corporations, organizations, and special-interest groups. Custom imprinting or excerpting can also be done to fit special needs. For information, please email specialmarketscms@penguinrandomhouse.com.

*To Benji. There is no one I would rather walk*
*with through the waves of this life.*
*Thank you for always pointing me*
*back to the Father.*

# CONTENTS

# SAFE
# ALL
# ALONG

# 1

## THE VIEW FROM ABOVE

When you pass through the waters,
    I will be with you;
and when you pass through the rivers,
    they will not sweep over you.

—ISAIAH 43:2

Our family stood on the banks of the Nile River, one of our favorite places to be, relax, and adventure. The rush of the rapids, the breeze off the water, the laughter, and an occasional shriek from one of our children carried up the riverbank, and I stood in awe, deeply grateful for all that God had carried us through over the past two years to bring us to this spot.

My husband, Benji, and I had sent seven children to college on a different continent, where they were navigating new cultures and foreign lifestyles, with an ocean and eight or nine hours of time difference between us. We had added another baby to our crew, which now totaled fifteen children, teens, and young adults. We had faced more than one medical emergency that left every member of our family reeling and had us traveling back and forth all over the place and spending more time apart than together. Like many other people, we had endured nine months of our country being fully locked down due to a global pandemic. And really, these are only a few of the things that were going on, added to the daily grind of just being humans trying to love each other and our neighbors well, trying to navigate online schooling and Zoom meetings and how to get groceries while not being allowed to drive a car due to pandemic restrictions in Uganda.

And now, for the first time in more than a year, we were together.

Needless to say, a family camping trip along our favorite river, at a section we'd never explored before, seemed like a needed reprieve. As our children get older and venture out into all corners of the world, I am keenly aware that our times of all being in one place are increasingly rare, and I purposed to soak up every minute. We were ready for adventure.

Almost all our family members are strong swimmers and decent kayakers, so even in new places along the river, I don't usually worry too much. On this day, as we stood with our kids at the edge of the little bay, the current looked strong, no doubt, but it also looked somewhat circular, as though you could get in and swim or float a bit and it would circle around and spit you back out near the shore. This is what we were banking on anyway. The thing about rivers is that you can't possibly tell how strong the current is until you're in it.

Ignoring the sign warning even strong swimmers *not to swim there,* Benji and one of our teenage daughters strapped on life jackets and jumped into the water. The current did exactly what we thought it would. They swam around and then let the circular tide bring them right back in to where the rest of us were standing. *Looks easy enough,* I thought, and I convinced our daughter to go again with me.

Another thing about rivers: They aren't exactly predictable. About halfway around the bend, the water shifted. Just thirty seconds later, we found ourselves fighting the current, swimming with all our strength toward the shore but instead being pushed farther away.

I called to our daughter, "Are you okay? Keep swimming!"

And she would answer, "Yeah, I'm okay!" with her head barely bobbing above the snow-white foam.

But I was beginning to feel desperate to get out of the water, and to get her out with me. I could hear Benji's voice in my head remarking that if we were to get caught up in the current (which, of course, we were sure that we would *not*), the tree sticking out from the shore at the edge of the bay would be our last chance to get out and we wouldn't want to let the current take us much farther due to the falls a little ways up the river.[1] I know. As I type this story out, the whole thing really doesn't sound like a good idea. But we are kind of an audacious group.

From my view in the water, the "last chance" tree was getting rapidly closer. And as it did, my panic rose. Everything in me swam for that tree. I kept calling out to my daughter (probably more to re-assure myself), who was farther out in the water than I was, "It's going to be okay! You can do it. Swim hard!" I craned my neck to see her as I swam with all my might. We were going to make it. As I reached my right hand out toward her, I used my other one to grab for an overhanging branch.

The limb snapped off in my hand.

I felt like I was watching myself in some kind of movie scene, willing myself to make it to the shore and somehow get my daughter there with me. The current crashed my legs against jagged rocks, still pulling my body fast, away from the bank I was reaching for, and still pulling my baby fast and away from my outstretched arm.

As I finally grabbed hold of another branch, I turned to reach for my daughter. But she was too far away, her arms outstretched, her head barely visible over the white foam of the rapids. I thought I heard her call for me as she was swept around the corner, out of my view, into the vast swirling water.

I know what you are thinking: *a mother's worst nightmare.* And it was. Had this been a scene from a movie, I couldn't have scripted it to be more intense. The current was still slamming my legs into the craggy shore as I clung, breathless, to my tree branch. Only one word came to my mind and to my lips: *Jesus.*

I'm not quite sure now, looking back, if I was actually yelling it or only crying out in my mind, over and over, *Jesus, Jesus, save her! Please, Jesus.* I had no idea what was around that bend in the river. Benji had mentioned falls up ahead, but I didn't know how far, and all I could do was imagine the worst. *Jesus, I need You to save my baby. I need You to save her, Lord Jesus. Please. Please. Please.* Over and over.

I realized I was still pulling hard on a tree limb that might not support my weight much longer. Slowly, I pulled myself up onto a boulder in the beating sun. Though later I realized that I was covered in cuts and bruises, I didn't remember feeling any pain. The sound of the river roared in my ears as I situated myself and waved to Benji and the girls far away on the shore, trying to somehow let them know that I was all right but that I was also *alone.* I was too far away to make out the expressions on their faces, and I wasn't sure how much they had been able to see.

No one seemed to be moving very frantically (though I later learned that a few of them had run up to get help from someone at the campsite), and I wondered why no one was screaming or crying in horror at the fact that I had surely just lost their sister to the raging rapids. I tried yelling to them that I couldn't see her and she wasn't safe, but the rushing water drowned out my voice. A few of them waved back, seemingly unfazed.

As I watched my family walking toward me, I never stopped calling out to Jesus to save our daughter. I don't know how long I sat there. It felt like a blink and also an eternity. It was certainly long enough to envision every possible worst-case scenario. I chided myself for being so foolish and overconfident and not heeding the warning of the sign. My mind filled with thoughts of having to search the river for a body. I sat on my rock, exhausted from both the river and the flood of emotions, and I prayed.

And then as Benji and the girls approached from my left through the bushes, another set of footsteps came running from a different path to the right. I caught a glimpse of her yellow swimsuit. I heard her voice. There she was!

She ran toward me and I shouted her name as she stumbled into my arms. "Are you okay?" I yelled, even though my face was right next to hers. "I thought I'd lost you. I thought you were gone! Are you okay?"

"Yeah, I'm okay!" she chuckled nonchalantly. "Some fishermen came and pulled me out. They were getting out of the water with their boat, but I called for them and they came back to get me. They put me on the shore just over there."

*Fishermen?* I briefly wondered. *People don't fish in water this fast.* I hadn't seen any fishermen or fishing boats on this stretch of the water our entire trip (and I didn't see any after that day either).

"I'm so sorry," I kept repeating. I was hugging her too tight. I finally pulled myself away to look into her eyes. "Were you so scared?" I asked.

"Nah." She shrugged. "I just kept thinking, *I'll find another way out.*"

And she bounded off, laughing with her sisters, joking that they were done swimming for the day.

I held it together for another minute as the rest of our girls called out to me, "You okay, Mom?" before heading back to camp. But when I got midway up the hill and found my husband's embrace, I let myself fall apart.

"I couldn't reach her," I sobbed. "I couldn't get to her. I lost her. I thought I lost her."

"It's all right. She's okay. You're okay," he whispered.

We stood like that for a long time while my breathing slowed and I let my panic fade. Then, ever gentle and kind, Benji took my hand. "Come on. Let me show you something."

He led me to the top of the riverbank, where I could see, way down below, my life-saving little tree sticking out just before the river opened up into all its glory—roaring, wide and expansive. We walked farther up, to a place I couldn't have seen when I was in the water. As we stood looking out, Benji pointed to all the additional places our daughter would have been able to get out had the fishermen not pulled her to safety. There was a tiny island she might have been able to swim over to. There was a break in the current where she could have headed toward the next little bay. Long before the falls, which turned out to be more than half a mile away, there were several calm places where someone could have gotten out of the current and to safety. He said, "Sure, some of these routes might have made it more difficult and a lot more time-consuming for you to get back to us at camp, but I knew you both would be all right."

The fishermen were behind our miraculous rescue that day, and I will forever believe that God sent them specifically for us. But from the top, looking out at the whole picture, it was clear that even if He hadn't sent those fishermen, He had also provided many other paths to rescue.

Immediately, it all felt incredibly safe again. My recent fear and panic seemed silly and unnecessary. I had grabbed the branch of a tree, imagining that the worst was right around the corner, but even if I hadn't, there would have been a number of routes to safety. Our daughter had been rescued by people and a boat, but now, seeing the whole map of the river's twists and turns, I knew she would have been fine regardless.

I stood there for a long time that day, watching the river. The water level rose and fell as the day went on. Sometimes the current spiraled furiously, and sometimes it was much more calm. The same phrase kept dropping into my mind as I looked out at what I had once thought to be perilous: *We were safe all along.*

Later that evening, I snapped a photo of the rushing current in the bay. Once again, it appeared to flow in a circular motion, right back to the shore, but I knew better. Each time I look at that picture, I praise God for His provision in the fishermen that day, reminded that He saved both me and my daughter from the waves. As I look at that image, a sense of peace washes over me. At eye level, it appeared that we were in grave danger, chaos surrounding us, but from up above it was clear: We were safe in the rushing river, guarded by a God who could see the whole picture and had a good plan. The Lord, our savior.

⌒

WE DIDN'T GET back in the river on that trip—well, at least not in that same spot. Now that I had seen the whole river with all its many currents from above, from high up on the riverbank, it felt completely safe, with many ways out and various opportunities to rest. I almost wanted to try swimming in there again, with the new confidence I had that we would be all right. I thought of how much I would have actually enjoyed the adrenaline rush of the rapid water if I had been certain we would get out safely. But I kept reminding myself how it had felt to be eye level with the waves, and I knew I would be completely unnerved if I tried to do it again. Instead, we moved upriver a few miles and found a still place to paddleboard and kayak and swim.

For many weeks after, I kept reliving my fear as the water crashed around me, as I watched my beloved child swept around the river bend out of my sight. Then I'd remember my relief when I changed perspectives and could see the river from above, the whole picture.

I realized it isn't so different for the difficult seasons that we inevitably pass through in this life. Caught up in the storms and rapids of challenging circumstances, with the waves at eye level, our scary or uncertain situations often seem impossible to escape. We can feel sure that this will be the end of us, that this will be the thing we will not overcome. From inside the current, we can see only a very small piece of the river, and it *is* scary.

But I imagine that for God it looks a whole lot more like what I saw standing on the edge of the riverbank with Benji, realizing that we had always been safe, that there had been so many different places to get out. God sees the whole picture: all the twists and turns, the places where the rapids swirl, the places of calm where we could swim lazily, the islands and tree branches that provide a place to rest, the people along the way who provide encouragement. He sees the whole trajectory of our lives, and He sees all that He is doing in each situation, working all things for good,[2] even in the midst of something that doesn't look good.

I reflected on the past few years for our family, all we had endured and all the situations I'd thought might take us under, tear our family apart, or completely destroy any good thing we had worked for. There were times when I thought my faith might be completely wrecked and I wondered how I would keep holding on. In the middle of those hardships, I couldn't have ever imagined that we would be here, together, healing, laughing, and worshipping God, who had carried us through. Even when we couldn't see it, even when we felt sure the rapids of life would pull us under, we were safe in His hands.

"My flesh and my heart may fail," says the psalmist, "but God is the strength of my heart and my portion forever."[3] When my strength, my heart, my faith, my whole life seemed to fail, God held me safe.

As He says through the prophet Isaiah,

Do not fear, for I have redeemed you;
　　I have summoned you by name; you are mine.
When you pass through the waters,
　　I will be with you;

and when you pass through the rivers,
　　they will not sweep over you.
When you walk through the fire,
　　you will not be burned;
　　the flames will not set you ablaze.
For I am the LORD your God,
　　the Holy One of Israel, your Savior.[4]


I can add nothing but my testimony: God is who He says He is, and when we cannot hold on any longer, He will not let go. He will carry us.

If you do not know Jesus and have made it this far, I am so glad you are here. It is my bold prayer that you would meet Him in these pages. I pray that you would know Him to be a God who is not just an authority but a dear friend, a God who not only sees but understands your pain and came to die so that you may one day be free from all pain and suffering. If I could, I would pat the seat next to me on the couch and beckon you to come. And I would grab your hand, dear one, and tell you that He wants you, He is wildly and urgently pursuing you, and the greatest desire of His tender heart is for you to intimately know Him and be known by Him, to experience the deep abounding peace that only He can offer. That is why He came. That is why He died.

The peace I experienced after I had seen our path from high above on the shore was completely opposite the panic I had felt as I was tossed and thrown by the waves. In the same way, the joy I felt to be out in His amazing creation with my family stood in stark contrast to the chaos and anxiety that had often colored the past few years. At eye level, the circumstances of our lives were overwhelming, but from far above, it was beautiful.

For the rest of our trip, as I looked out at the river, I imagined different ways I might have approached our trials of the past many years if I had seen it all in advance and known that we would be here together and that our lives would not be utterly ruined or irreparably broken. And I thought of the peace that would be mine if I could go through life having first seen the view from above, the entire plan. If I could see all the ways that hard things would grow me and strengthen my faith and if I could be certain that at the end we really would all be okay. What if—even as the waters of life rose around me, around my loved ones—I could live in the confidence I'd known that day on the bank that we were indeed safe all along?

I know, both from experience and from what I read in Scripture, that though my family and I have faced our fair share of hardships, and certainly will again, none of us will ever be outside the reach of God, who sees the whole plan from above, who knows exactly what He is doing and where we are going.

And I want desperately to learn how to live in the certainty of this truth. I want to live in a peace that is dependent not on my circumstance but on the unchanging character of my God.

I didn't know it yet on that trip, but He would soon move us into a season just as challenging as the one before. Illness and crisis would once again rear their ugly heads in our family. Lockdown would end but restart shortly after with the onset of a new Covid-19 variant. We would again walk with friends and neighbors who were starving, desperate, without jobs and basic provisions, and often without hope. We would find ourselves unexpectedly living in a new country, on a new continent, for an indefinite period of time, deeply grieving a life that we adored and a place we had expected to call home for years to come, deeply lonely in ways we had never experienced. And just as before, we wouldn't be able to see the whole plan, to know what was coming next or what was around the bend.

I believe that the Lord is intentional in not allowing us to see the whole plan or know the ending. Though those few minutes on the rock were excruciating, I can remember only a handful of other times when I have cried out to Him with such urgency. Because I couldn't see the whole story, I called out to Jesus as if my life, and my daughter's, depended on it.

But I don't want to move through life as the panicked, fearful woman I was in the rapids. I want to live as the steady version of myself who stood on the riverbank rather than the frantic version of myself caught in the waves. I want to call out to Jesus as if my life depends on it, because it does, and I want to do so with the certainty that He will, He has, rescued us. I want to be a steady, unanxious person of prayer not just for my own mental, emotional, and spiritual health but for my family, my community, and all those who might catch a glimpse of Christ through me. I want to live out of the place of peace that Jesus promises.

"Peace I leave with you," Jesus says,[5] but if I am honest, in the midst of life's rapids, the trials and the hardship and the hurt, as the waters rise and the fire blazes, peace is hard for my heart and mind to grasp. After our encounter at the river, I began to earnestly study peace and ask God for it. I don't want to just know what the peace of Christ is; I want to live in the confidence and security that God has promised me. I want to be both desperate for Him and deeply anchored in His certain peace as the world around me spins in chaos.

Maybe you do too? I believe that in Christ this is possible. And I believe we can learn together. We can learn to truly believe that He sees all our days and allows the scary and uncertain situations only as a means to draw us to Him, to cause us to cry out desperately for Him and lean into Him in new ways. We can walk in the confidence we might have if we could see the ending, *even though we can't*. We can learn to live in the steady assurance that in Christ, we are safe all along.

# 2

## PULLED APART

He saw the disciples straining at the oars, because the wind was against them.

—MARK 6:48

Over the years, I've had many friends who struggle with feeling anxious. I tried to be sympathetic, but until I grappled with it myself, I had no idea how completely crippling anxiety can be.

Then, about two years before our stressful swim in the Nile, a family emergency took my husband halfway across the world, and he was able to send only irregular, disconnected updates about our loved one who was in crisis. An unfamiliar panic tied my stomach in knots and sent my mind spinning.

I pushed it away and tried to think straight. With a newborn, a toddler, and a slew of teenagers to parent, I didn't have time to fall apart. I took to hiding in the bathroom, away from the watching eyes of my children, just long enough to compose myself and control my suddenly rapid breathing. I tossed and turned in bed, physically exhausted as my mind spun with worrying what-ifs. After a few months, our loved one got better (or so we thought), my husband returned, and I successfully willed myself to be poised, calm, steady.

Until another crisis hit.

My husband noticed it first, the way I couldn't stop bouncing my leg at the dinner table, how I could no longer make a decision without hours or sometimes days of deliberation, only to repeatedly question myself once a decision was made. My mind was again spinning out of control, and my body followed suit. My heart was thumping too fast, and my stomach seemed continually on the verge of nausea.

I was frustrated. I knew all the "right answers," the things I "should" do to calm my mind and body. I read books that promised to give me a solution. I spoke to myself about how God was in control and how it would be all right in the end. I prayed, repeatedly asking Him to take this feeling away. I chided myself for my lack of faith, as if I somehow could muster up enough trust in God that this would all go away.

But my leg still bounced up and down, almost involuntarily, anytime I sat for a few minutes. I still felt like my mind was agitated, uneasy, unsteady. And I still found myself exhausted but wide awake in the middle of the night, staring at the ceiling and imagining every worst-case scenario.

The truth is that the anxiety had probably been there for a very long time, but for years I had been able to mask it with my favorite addiction: busyness. I had moved to Uganda in my very early adulthood to volunteer, and during my time there, God led me to found a ministry, Amazima, which grew rapidly as people came alongside to help serve our community. Years before I married Benji, I also began the process to adopt thirteen of our fifteen children. With a large family and a large ministry, plus a host of other responsibilities and tasks, I found that it had become easy, even natural, to bury my emotions for the sake of keeping everything going. But even while I presented myself as strong and composed, the anxiety, though unnamed, would come out sideways, perhaps through my snapping at my kids or feeling totally overwhelmed by a fairly simple task or decision.

Have you felt it too? Activity and productivity and false security in success or circumstances can cover it for a while, but deep down our hearts are desperate. *Our flesh always wants to keep pushing through, but our hearts need to rest in our Father.*

For me, the distraction of busyness and the disguise of mere irritation could no longer conceal the truth. I was anxious, about almost everything, and I hated it. I didn't like this frantic, shaky, hesitant person I had slowly become, and I was unsure how I got there or how to get back to the confident, decisive person I once was.

Around this time, a good friend asked how I was doing, and I decided to just go for it and be honest. "It seems silly to complain with so many around us obviously suffering more than we are," I said. "I know we are unbelievably blessed. But I just feel anxious, defeated . . . *exhausted.* I'm worried about everything, which is so unlike me, and it just leaves me plain worn out."

There. I had finally gathered the courage to say aloud the thought that had been swirling in my mind for weeks, maybe months—the thought that I had repeatedly told myself was ridiculous. I waited for my friend to shake her head at me. I had just gotten back from vacation, for crying out loud. I was suntanned and freshly manicured and was supposed to feel relaxed from a few days away on the ocean. But the moment I re-entered "real life," my head started to spin with a million decisions to make, a million conversations to have, a million problematic scenarios that hadn't even happened yet. Although my body was rejuvenated, my brain and my heart were tired. Deeper than tired. *Weary.*

Instead of being exasperated, my friend reached her hand over and placed it on my knee. "I am so thankful you said that," she said with a little gasp. "I am so glad that I am not the only one who feels this way! This is exactly how I have been feeling for weeks."

*Me too.* It's amazing how validating those two little words can be for a weary soul.

Over the course of the next several months, as I braved vulnerability and shared my weariness and thought battles with a few other
trusted friends, I was surprised to hear all of them say exactly that:
*Me too.*

It wasn't just me. And it wasn't just a few of my trusted friends. It
seems like in some ways everyone is spinning. Individually and collectively, we are weary. We are uncertain. We feel a little untethered.
We are bombarded with information, so much of it negative or scary.
We observe injustice and war and dramatically increasing insecurity
and unsafety in events taking place around the world. Racism. Vio-
lence. Homelessness. Economic volatility. Things are hard and seemingly getting harder. As I shared my anxiety and exhaustion with
other women I know and trust, here are some of the things I heard:

- "I cannot make one more decision."
- "I am just always beating myself up."
- "I am worried all the time."
- "My stomach is tied up in knots just thinking about what is
  next."
- "I don't think I am really contributing anything."
- "I feel like a failure."
- "I'm just afraid that nothing is going to work out the way I
  planned."
- "This isn't how I thought it would go."
- "This isn't where I thought I would be by now."
- "I think I have forgotten how to look forward to anything."
- "I feel . . . hopeless."

I identified with every single one of these statements. I thought,
*Yes, I feel this way too.* Yet at the same time, I also knew this isn't who
God created me to be. This isn't who He created any of us to be.

We see repeatedly in Scripture how God calls us to live in steadfast confidence, to be people who live in the peace of Christ and carry it to others:

- "God has not given us a spirit of fear, but of power and of love and of a sound mind."[1]
- "Do not be anxious about anything."[2]
- "Let the peace of Christ rule in your hearts."[3]
- "Do not worry about your life."[4]
- "Cast all your anxiety on him because he cares for you."[5]

The Greek word in the New Testament that is translated as "worry" or "anxiety" in a few of the verses above is *merimna,* and it indicates being pulled apart, divided into parts, or pulled in opposite directions.[6] When I first read this definition, it resonated deeply. That described exactly how I was feeling: torn to pieces. As my mind raced ahead to all the what-ifs of tomorrow, next month, and next year, I was unable to be present in today. My attention was torn away from what God had set in front of me as I tried to control the outcomes of days that had not yet even taken shape, days that are not even promised to me.

At the same time, my thoughts frequently fixated on regrets over past decisions or conversations. *If I had just done this differently,* or *If I had just said this instead.* Again, I was being torn away from the peace God was offering me right here, right now.

Maybe you can relate. Maybe the pain of life just keeps knocking you down, leaving you exhausted and anxious. Maybe, like me, you are trying to hold it all together for the sake of those around you. Trying to give everyone and everything the best you have, even when you don't have much left and you are feeling weary. Trying to show up for those you love and care about.

You and I aren't the only ones. Our churches, neighborhoods, and families are marked by miscarriage and infertility, affairs and marriage struggles, wayward children and lost children and sick children. Sick and aging parents. Scary diagnoses. Joblessness. Homelessness. *Hopelessness.*

So many of us are trying to put on a strong face for the sake of the rest of the world while inwardly we are falling apart. We are letting our circumstances and emotions lead the way instead of internalizing the truth of God's ability to make a way. Like me, in the waves, we are calling out to those around us, "You are okay! Keep going," when inwardly we are panicked, drowning in fear. We long to return to the steady, confident people we once were, or maybe we long to be steady and confident for the first time.

If you are feeling this way, first of all I want to bring you in close

## TOGETHER IN THE BOAT

Do you identify with the anxious struggles of so many of my friends? Take a moment to stop and examine what feels like a storm in your life right now, where you feel anxious, fearful, weary, exhausted, or hopeless. In what area of your life do you feel like you are straining against the wind, making no progress? Write these things down and invite Jesus to "join you in the boat," to enter into the struggle and sit in it with you.

Spend some time in silence listening for the voice of Jesus that says, "Take courage! It is I. Don't be afraid." We can begin here and now to open our hearts to Jesus, who sees us, who comes to us, who joins us in the struggle, climbing into the boat with us to shoulder our burdens and calm our anxious hearts.

and assure you I'm not here to hand out guilt or blame but to offer a life raft of hope. Jesus is not disappointed in you, but He has something better for you.

I also want to acknowledge that you may be dealing with a clinical anxiety disorder, depression, or some other real, chemical mental illness. This is not the same thing as worry. There is a difference between situational anxiety or nervousness about the future and a true chemical disorder. While the anxiety I battled in the recent season of my life was mostly situational—the residue of pain, loss, and trauma that had blindsided my family, compounded by lingering exhaustion from ministry—I know many amazing Christians who trust God with their whole hearts and still struggle with depression, anxiety, or other mental illness that requires medical intervention. *You are not alone.*

As I type this, I am seeing a counselor weekly and taking antidepressants to help combat the low-grade sadness that I have experienced for my entire adult life. I believe both are gifts the Lord uses to help me be at my best for myself, my family, and others I serve. These things undergird the tangible habits I have intentionally put in place to help myself and my family learn to lean into the deep peace Jesus offers.

If you are struggling in a similar way, I am so sorry. I see you. This is not your fault, and it does not make you less faithful. There is no shame in seeking the help you need through therapy or medication or both. As I venture to share some things God has used to help me with my own battle with anxiety, I would never want to suggest that simply thinking differently or forming new habits will be a "fix-all." He sends "fishermen" to help us on our journey, and therapists have often been mine.

That said, as I have studied God's promised peace, longing to not only claim it for myself but also be a vessel offering it to others, He has given me some practices that help me stay more grounded and steady, more certain in Him even as the world around me spins in chaos. Just because the world is spinning and pulled apart doesn't mean my mind has to be. Along with those practices, which we'll explore later and which I'm still learning to apply consistently, God offered His abundant grace in exchange for my self-condemnation, my tendency to believe I should be stronger than this. When I felt that it was too hard to hold on to Him and His peace, our faithful God held on to me.

AS I PRAYED through some of the things I was wrestling with in my own life—worry, control, exhaustion, overwhelm—and questioned whether my wrestling indicated a lack of faithfulness on my part, I felt that the Lord led me to Mark 6.

In this passage, Jesus sends His twelve disciples out to work and teach.[7] They take no provisions along as they travel through the surrounding region, healing the sick, casting out demons, staying at the homes of any strangers who will take them. They are on mission, faithfully doing as Jesus instructed.

While they are away, their friend John the Baptist is killed.[8] As the disciples gather together and report to Jesus all they have done, they must be exhausted, sad, and maybe afraid that they could be killed for this work too. The Scripture says that so many people are coming and going that they don't even have a chance to eat. They are *weary.* And they aren't tired and weary because they are doing something wrong or because of a lack of faithfulness or obedience; they are tired and weary because they are doing *exactly what Jesus has instructed them to do.* Jesus seems to recognize this too and beckons them to come away with Him to a quiet place to get some rest. He *wants* them to be restored.

But before they can get anywhere quiet, a crowd surrounds them. There is more work to be done. And in typical Jesus fashion, even though He longs to rest with the ones He loves, even though He is probably grieving deeply the loss of His cousin and friend, when He sees people in need, He lingers with them. He teaches them. He feeds them. He asks His disciples to do the same.

We often focus on the miracle of this story: that Jesus was able to feed thousands upon thousands of people with five loaves of bread and two fish.[9] I love this clear picture of God as our provider, and I am reminded of it often when my own family is in need of provision. But as the Lord prompted me to read it with fresh eyes, all I could think about was how tired the disciples, and even Jesus, must have been. They were on their way to *rest* from weeks of hard ministry and were interrupted, yet again, to serve. And that isn't the end of it. Right after they feed the thousands, before they even have a chance to nap, Jesus sends His disciples on ahead of Him to their next stop so that He can be alone to pray. Their eyelids heavy, their limbs aching, the disciples climb into the boat, only to face a windstorm in the middle of the night.[10] The text doesn't say how long the disciples were straining at the oars, pushing against the wind, but it does say that they were *making no headway.*

Have you felt like this? I identified so deeply with the disciples as I battled my own anxiety and spiraling thoughts. I felt like I was doing what I was supposed to be doing, but I wasn't making any headway. I was tired. I was stuck.

And I felt that God was showing me that we can be tired and we can be stuck *even when we have been faithful.* It isn't some kind of failure on my part or yours that led us to this anxious place; it is simply the state of our fallen, broken world. All of us, like the disciples, are just fighting, with the wind against us, to hold on and do our best by the people we love. And I gained encouragement from the way Jesus approached the disciples that night in the boat.

They were stuck. They were straining. They were exhausted. They couldn't find their way through. *And Jesus went out to them.*

Friend, He comes to you and me in our struggles.

In our stuck places. In our dark, anxious, hopeless places.

And Jesus didn't just go to them; *He spoke to them.* "Take courage! It is I. Don't be afraid."[11] *Peace.* He speaks to us in our sadness, in our panic, in our frantic grasping for control, telling us that we do not have to be afraid.

And then *He climbed into the boat with them.*

I want you to pause here for a moment and close your eyes. I don't know what is hard for you today or what you are struggling with. Whatever you are battling, whatever feels scary or impossible, I want you to imagine Jesus joining you in it. He promises that He will. He gets in the boat with you. You are never in the boat alone.

I hope you find as much comfort and reassurance in this truth as I did. My anxiety didn't show up overnight, and it wasn't going to go away overnight. But here was Jesus, coming for me, talking to me, and joining me in the darkest places, where I was stuck and straining, speaking encouragement to my heart when I was tired and weary and struggling. And as I began to truly believe that I wasn't navigating this alone, I also began to learn what it looks like to move toward peace.

Whenever I felt anxiety pulling at my heart and mind, I would think of Jesus entering the boat with the disciples and I would allow myself to pause and hear His words: "Take courage! It is I. Don't be afraid." When my emotions wanted to take charge, I returned to the Word of God, remembering what is true and picturing Jesus calming the gale-force wind of my feelings.

When Jesus got into the boat with the disciples, another miraculous thing happened: The wind stopped. Is it possible? Could we learn to be so in tune with Him that even when we are stuck, we are not afraid? That though the waves of the world crash around us, we could feel our hearts grow calm as we gaze upon our savior? I think so. In fact, I know so.

First Peter 5:7 instructs us to cast all our anxieties on Jesus because He cares for us. We *can* cast all our anxieties on Him because He is in the boat with us. We can live as people who have the spirit of power, love, and a sound mind promised to us in Him.[12] We can trust our lives and our futures to a good God who cares for His people and draws near to them in their times of need. A God who comes to us, a God who speaks to us, a God who joins us in our trials and promises to give us His perfect peace.

A God who has sought us and loved us from the moment of the world's creation.

# 3

## AS IT WAS IN THE BEGINNING

Did God really say, "You must not eat from any tree in the garden"?

—GENESIS 3:1

I think I first fell in love with Benji as I sat on the rickety metal bench of the local hospital and listened to him teach from Genesis 1. If I ever need to fall in love with the Word of God all over again, this is where I start. But let me back up a little further.

When I initially moved to Uganda, I was thrilled to be there and was constantly in awe of all the new sights, sounds, smells, and experiences. I was also deeply lonely. Because I was the only American and one of the only English speakers at the orphanage where I lived for a while, it was easy to feel isolated even while developing new and beautiful friendships. As I prayed for God to give me a community, He led me to invite a small group of like-minded people, both expats and Ugandans, into my home on Wednesday nights for a Bible study.

We started small. We were all young, we were all passionate about Jesus, and for the most part, none of us had any idea what we were doing. But every Wednesday, we showed up. We came exhausted and overwhelmed. We shared our failures and our triumphs and everything in between. Because most of us were involved in ministry of some kind, it wasn't unusual for one or more of us to get stuck at the local hospital on a Wednesday night, or any night. And without fail, if one of our own was there, our little Bible study would move from the cracked-tile floor of my living room to the cold cement courtyard of the clinic so that we could keep vigil and fellowship at the same time.

The hospital we gathered at was by far the best available option in our small town. Still, if you had a patient or loved one there, you had to stay by their side around the clock to ensure they got the care they needed. Often one or two doctors or nurses managed entire wards of patients, all with varying and severe needs. Patients slept on rusty metal beds, and caretakers on the floor beside them. Sometimes the correct medicine was available; sometimes it wasn't, and the only thing to do was sit beside patients and comfort them while they waited. Outside the wards of the hospital was a small patio lined with uncomfortable metal benches where caretakers could sit to get some air or just take a break from the constant smell of sickness inside the rooms.

This was the scene on the night we decided to invite the new guy in town to lead our study. Benji taught the creation story in a way I hadn't heard it before, and I still think of it often. It would be three years before I said yes to a date, and almost two more before I said yes to being his wife, but that night, listening to him made the Word of God come alive. Something in my heart was captivated.

As our group sat under the stars on the unsteady benches and listened, Benji read from the very first lines of his Bible: "In the beginning God created the heavens and the earth. Now the earth was formless and empty, darkness was over the surface of the deep."[1] Benji asked us to close our eyes and imagine complete and total chaos. In the chilly night, with the sounds of machines beeping and nurses shuffling and patients groaning in the background, chaos and darkness seemed near, palpable, easy to imagine. The weight of ministry to those who were hurting felt tangible, our exhaustion thick in the open air.

"Now, I want you to imagine," his steady, strong voice continued, "the Spirit of God hovering near. The Word says, 'And the Spirit of God was hovering over the waters.'[2] God is here. He is near to our dark and our chaos. He is hovering right here with a plan and a purpose."

You probably know the line that comes next.

"And God said, 'Let there be light,' *and there was light.*"[3]

Can't you just imagine the way it shattered the darkness?

And even though I'd read that passage tens, maybe hundreds, of times in my twenty-two years of life, it hit me differently that night as I imagined God hovering near to our chaos, near to our pain, near to our darkness with His good plan and purpose.

If you are at all familiar with this part of the Bible, you know that God goes on to create a beautiful and perfect world out of nothing, and as He creates each element and piece of this home, He declares it all good. And last but not least, He creates people in His own image.

The Bible and the entire universe begin with God's life-giving peace. He comes near to chaos and disorder and speaks light into the dark, peace and order into a chaotic void, and life into His creation. He reverses disorder and brings about the whole world, weaving ultimate tranquility and beauty into every aspect of its perfection. I imagine God preparing all of creation for the beloved children He is about to breathe into life.

I remember, years after that first evening of studying Scripture with the man I would marry, preparing for the arrival of our first son. Setting up the crib and arranging things just right. Washing and folding tiny onesies and organizing miniscule diapers with such great anticipation of who this little life kicking inside me would be. Since I would be giving birth at home, Benji and I gathered supplies—towels, washcloths, tiny blankets—in preparation for the amazing day when we would welcome him into the world. I think of how it delights me, each time we move, to set up our girls' rooms just right, making sure they have everything they need to feel comfortable in a new place. I imagine this is only a tiny glimpse of how God felt as He designed His beautiful, perfect world for the children He was about to create to share it with.

So, too, in the beginning, our loving Father created every tree and plant, every bird and beast, light, food, water, the perfect home to bring His children into, the perfect way to point them back to His glory time and time again. Everything held together in perfect unity.

By the time God finally created man and woman in His own image and blessed them and instructed them, He had already given them everything they would need for life with Him in the garden. Earth and sky and waters teeming with fish, fruits, and plants in abundance, light to make the seasons and the days, to warm their skin and light their paths.

Imagine the sense of rest and certainty you feel when you know that you have exactly what you need for the day ahead. *That* is what God's creation was born into. Imagine the great satisfaction of God when He saw all the beauty He'd created and declared it so good. And now imagine Him gazing on His very favorite part: His children.

Benji and I often put our kids to bed only to sit in our own bed and tell stories of all the darling things they've done throughout the day, frequently pulling out our phones to show one another photos and videos we have taken. "She is just so precious," we will say. "I can't believe how fast he is learning!" We have spent the whole day with them, and we have sent them to their own rooms just so we can be alone together, yet we sit and dote, amazed by these humans we get to shepherd and shape. Sure, they are far from perfect, but I doubt you'd know it if you heard our late-night conversations or saw the delight in our eyes as we watch the video of the baby saying bye-bye for the hundredth time.

In this way, I imagine God sits back and declares His creation good, His children beloved. There they stand, naked and unashamed

## WHERE ARE YOU?

Take time to honestly ask and answer the question "Where are you?" Do you feel close to God in this season or far from Him? Are there places you feel naked and exposed from shame? Places where you know you have messed up and you feel that somehow you can hide it from Him?

Unrepented sin is often a place where I find myself hiding. I am just not ready to let go of something yet, so I don't bring it into the light of my prayer life.

- Where are you hiding?
- What areas of your life feel just a little too precious, a little too fragile, to fully surrender to the Lord?
- What parts of you are feeling pulled apart by anxiety?
- Where are you feeling strong in Him? Where are you doubting His goodness?
- Where are you questioning Him?
- Where do you feel that He has let you down? Where do you feel that you have let *Him* down?
- What are you hoping for? Where are you rejoicing?

As we move into our quest for God's promised peace, we can take comfort in knowing He sees, knows, and holds all that is in our hearts!

in front of their loving Father, just as He created them to be, His delight abounding in them and theirs in Him.

Surely *this* is the picture of perfect peace, perfect rest, perfect certainty: God's children basking in the love of the Creator and Father, walking in unhindered relationship with Him, not wondering for a second if their needs will be provided for.

From the very beginning, God has been the ultimate provider of our peace. But because humans were involved, this all came crashing down rather quickly. We don't know how long Adam and Eve enjoyed the paradise of the garden, but in the record of Genesis, it is just one chapter after they were created that their eyes began to lust after what they did not have, ultimately leading to the destruction of their tranquility.

There, right after the perfect beginning, is the crafty hiss of the serpent, God's enemy and ours. This is where it all begins to unravel. In case you don't know the full story, although God has given His creation everything they need for their perfect life with Him, He has also given them some parameters—well, just one really. They can eat the fruit of any tree in the garden *except one.* God gives this instruction as a protection for them; He knows that if they have a complete understanding of the knowledge of good and evil, suffering will enter His perfect world, and as a kind and merciful Father, He wouldn't be able to allow His children to live forever in a world of pain.

Adam and Eve don't seem to buck against this instruction initially, but the clever serpent hisses in Eve's ear the same lie that plagues us all today: "Did God really say 'You must not eat from *any* tree in the garden'?"[4]

You've heard it too, haven't you? That sneaky thought, that insidious whisper suggesting that maybe, just maybe God isn't giving you all you need—that maybe He's withholding something better from you.

"Did God really say . . ." it begins. "Would God really care about something so small?" or "God must not care if He won't let you have what you want" or "If God really did care, He would never allow this."

Notice how the serpent twists the truth, how the thing he asks Eve isn't truly an accurate reflection of what God said but it's close. At first she tries to fight it: "We *may* eat the fruit of the trees in the garden, but not the tree in the middle, lest we die."[5]

"You will not die," the serpent asserts.[6] His lies are appealing. And Eve believes the lie—the one I, too, am often quick to believe: *God withholds good from me. God does not give me what I need. I must go after it for myself.* I have thought it even when I didn't dare say it. Haven't you? I've thought that I must take matters into my own hands when God's plans don't *look* good, when they aren't quite what I want or exactly how I imagined. I have been Eve and believed that if God truly loved me, He would give me exactly what I want.

I see so much of myself in Eve, tempted to mistrust God, tempted to ignore His goodness. These past few years have been the most challenging and disorienting I have ever lived through. I've mentioned already the life-altering health crisis that hit one of our loved ones and sent all of us into a spiral. A series of extremely difficult events left us reeling and ultimately prompted us to move our family to the United States. At thirty-three years old, I had lived my entire adult life on the red dirt roads of beautiful Uganda, and with all its quirks and hardships, I *loved* living there, loved raising my family there. Though it seemed clear that God was leading our family to move for many reasons, my insides churned and tears welled up at the idea of leaving my home. *There must be some other way. Surely a loving God would grant my heart's desire.*

And in all the questioning and doubting, another message of the serpent slips in. "You can be like God," he says.[7] This is always the promise of our enemy, the false promise—that we can take things into our own hands, that we can know better, that we can be the god of our own lives. Haven't you felt the allure of control? We all believe it sometimes—that it would be better if *we* were in charge, that we might achieve more on our own, that our plan might be better, that we can decide what is right and wrong for ourselves.

"God withholds good from you," the serpent taunts, and Eve reaches out and takes a big juicy bite of the lie. She eats the fruit. She gives some to her husband too. They set their hearts to do what they want, dissatisfied with God and what He had given. Dissatisfied with the peace, wholeness, and completeness that He had already granted them.

And with those bites, things revert to disorder and chaos.

Adam and Eve notice their lack for the first time. They realize they are naked, and where they weren't ashamed before, now they are. They hear the sound of the Lord walking in the garden and they run to hide. *Merimna* pulls them apart, pulls them away from their perfect unity with the Creator.

Chaos, fear, isolation, *dissatisfaction.* The complete opposite of the peace that God desired to give His people and His world. And for generations to come, God's people would, and still do, feel the strain. We are pulled apart, pulled away from perfect unity with our God. Once the lie enters the world, it takes root. God's people continually question Him. *Is God really good? Should He have given us more? Is there something better?* The Israelites cry out for food in the desert, and after the divine manna is provided, they tire of it, tire of God's provision, and ask for meat.[8] God's people groan for hundreds of years for a savior, and when He comes down to earth, they ignore Him, ridicule Him, and ultimately crucify Him.[9] Greed and pride get the better of Adam and Eve, of the Israelites, and of us.

The Enemy still whispers. God's people still believe that we can do better, that we can control, that we can succeed alone. And realizing our lack, we still run and hide from our Father instead of running *to* the One who knows the depths of our hearts and still longs to hold us in His loving arms.

Do you feel it? Where are you being pulled away from God and the unity He longs to have with you? Where are you believing the Enemy's lies that things would be better if you could just control the situation yourself? I confess, control has been my idol, the apple I just keep biting into.

Maybe you have a grand and glorious plan for your life—for your children, your family, your work, your church—if God would just get on board with it. Maybe you feel you know exactly what would be best for you and your people and are frustrated or annoyed that God's plan doesn't seem to be lining up very well with your own. Maybe you are looking at your life and it isn't how you thought it would go and you are certain that you would be more satisfied, less anxious, more joyful if you could have things your way. I know. I've been there.

Have you, like Eve, like me, been tempted to believe that God is withholding good from you? Have you noticed the way this lie pulls us apart inside?

Here's the good news: We don't have to be ashamed. We can come out of hiding and be seen and known by a good Father who longs for unity with His people. We can unclench our fists and receive His mercy.

THERE ADAM AND Eve are. The people God created for Himself out of nothing, the people He created to love and be loved by Him, have defied and disobeyed Him, and embarrassed by their naked-ness and sin, they run and hide in the bushes.[10] It all sounds so famil-iar to my own rebellious heart. Yet merciful God comes looking for them. *He is always coming for us gently, always reaching for us, always finding us.*

For us who are lost.

For us who are broken.

For us who have tried and failed and tried and failed again.

For us who are ashamed.

"Why are you hiding?" He asks, but He already knows. "You ate from the tree, didn't you?"[11] He speaks to you like this too, you know. Can you imagine Him looking into your eyes? "Don't hide, love," He says. "I already know."

The God who formed and fashioned Adam and Eve to live forever with Him already knew that they would rebel against Him. And in His great loving-kindness, He already had a plan to save and redeem them too. Here in the garden, He spares our lives for the first time. Those He promised would surely die if they ate a bite of the fruit from that one tree go on to live another day. And another. They will die, eventually, but God already has in mind a plan to bring them back to His original design: life with Him forever. In His great mercy, He clothes their nakedness and still allows them breath in their lungs and the sun on their faces and the warm earth beneath their feet to grow food for their sustenance. It will be difficult, yes. It isn't the perfect world in the perfect way that God intended. But that doesn't change the fact that He continued (and continues!) to provide for His people.

"Where are you?" God asks; it's one of the first questions recorded in all of Scripture. But He doesn't ask it because He needs them to answer. He knows where they are. *He always knows where we are.* Maybe He asks it to let them know He is there.

*I'm staying right here. Where are you?*

As we begin this journey to receive the perfect peace that God longs to give us, that's a good question to begin with. *Where are you?* And wherever you are, God is there too. He is Immanuel, God with us, always right there with you. He is the God who hovered near to the chaos and determined to make it good. He is the God who stays with us in the rapids, the God who in the person of Jesus got in the boat amid the storm.

Even as God moves Adam and Eve out of the garden, He gives His people a promise. There is no human way out of the problem of sin and banishment from life in Eden with God. We can't do it ourselves. But He promises right away that one day the offspring of woman will indeed crush the head of the Enemy. *There will be a deliverer.*

> "Though the mountains be shaken
>     and the hills be removed,
> yet my unfailing love for you will not be shaken
>     nor my covenant of peace be removed,"
>     says the LORD, who has compassion on you.[12]

God covenants, promises, to give His people perfect, unshakable peace. He will love us no matter what. He will love us to death—the death of His Son.

Sin and Satan devastate God's peaceful world, but they do not ultimately win. God already has a plan to restore order and bring His people back to Himself.

Our God is coming for us. Our God has a plan to redeem us.

Into our hiding.

Into our doubt.

Into our questions.

Into our dissatisfaction.

Into our failures.

*He will send His Son.*

Jesus. *Immanuel.*

Peace isn't something we can produce through our own resources. It will have to be found in Jesus.

# 4

## THE SEARCH FOR SHALOM

*Peace I leave with you; my peace I give you.*

—JOHN 14:27

My friend Abigail exudes a calm confidence that is almost unfathomable to me, a peace that I deeply desire to know and live out of. I have learned more about Jesus from her than from anyone else I know.

We met fourteen years ago in a slum community of Uganda at a Bible study where Abigail first was translating and later was leading. Over the years, as we invited each other into our homes, lives, and hearts, a dear friendship formed. Abigail's oldest daughter and my oldest daughter are close in age, and our youngest sons are just months apart. We've been pregnant and having babies at the same times; we've faced similar struggles in parenting and ministry. While our lives are vastly different, mostly due to where we live, our hearts are wildly similar.

Several years ago, I was stunned to find out that Abigail planned to leave the town we were both living in and return to her hometown on the northern border of Uganda. It was a choice that boggled my mind. As if living in the slum on the outskirts of town wasn't challenging enough—with rampant crime and addiction, as well as lack of access to clean food and water, stable sources of income, or secure housing—she was willingly relocating her family of nine to the most impoverished region in all of Uganda, where famine and drought frequently swept through whole communities, where locusts ate entire years' worth of crops, where hospitals were hours away. As someone who loves her dearly, I worried. *Will she be able to get what she needs? Will she be able to grow food? Will her children be all right?*

When I asked why she would move there, Abigail's answer was simple and confident. "That's my home," she said, though she had lived elsewhere since she was fourteen. "I feel called to go and share the Gospel there. If I don't go, who will?"

Just like that, she bought a small plot of property in the dry and barren savanna, built a house out of sticks and mud, and moved her children and her mom into their small hut between their cattle pen and tiny garden.

Abigail's family frequently endures hardships that I will likely never know. Each year, they experience periods of drought, walking miles from home daily to fetch the water they need. Living far away from anything remotely like a grocery store or doctor's office, they are at continual risk of famine and disease. Each night as they lay their heads on the dirt floor of their home, they face the very real possibility that cattle raiders will come under cover of darkness and shoot them in order to steal their cows, the livelihood of the people of their region.

A few months after her move, as I planned a visit to Abigail and her family, I hesitantly asked via FaceTime, "But the cattle raiders . . . Is it really safe for me to bring the girls with me?"

I felt sheepish for even asking, for suggesting that maybe I should keep my children safe from the daily reality in which she raises hers. If she would answer that my children wouldn't be safe camping next to her house, she would also be admitting that her own children are not safe. She had already told me multiple stories of them hiding in their cornfields and praying as they watched the raiders' feet passing through their yard, as they heard the gunshots at their neighbors' homes.

"God who kept us safe before will keep us again," she said, her eyes glistening with a deep joy that can only come from the Holy Spirit.

*Of course,* I thought. *Of course that would be your answer.*

Year after year, I watch Abigail walk in the confidence that Jesus is all she needs and that He will take care of her. She trusts God far more than her own ability to control her circumstances or make sure things work out her way, and because of this, she exudes a peace that is otherworldly, a peace that I long to inhabit. She feels safe and secure amid life's rapids, even though she cannot see the view from above, because she fully believes and trusts that *God can.* She is unshakably confident in every situation and the direst of circumstances. And she would be the first to tell you that it is because of Christ who lives in her.

The apostle Paul says in Ephesians that Jesus Himself is our peace,[1] and I think therein lies Abigail's secret. We want our peace to come from the outside, and we wait for the waves to still so that we can grasp it. But any peace this world offers is momentary and fleeting. *True peace, Jesus's peace, transcends all circumstances because it is found only in Him and He remains unchanging.*

I think of the last few years, not just for me personally but for the entire world, and the idea of peace seems increasingly elusive. We are bombarded with illness, political unrest, and increasing oppression and division, not to mention the daily struggles in our own homes, and yes, peace feels far out of reach as the world spins in chaos. It seems like each time I personally, or we collectively, get close to coming up for air, we are hit by another family emergency or personal crisis or natural disaster or financial upheaval or . . . The list goes on.

On a smaller scale, when we think of peace, we tend to imagine a quiet day without kids squabbling with each other or clamoring for attention, relaxation in an idyllic mountain or beach setting, or perhaps a hot bubble bath in candlelit silence. Maybe we think of peace as life without chaos, a known schedule in the days ahead, a sense of control over our circumstances. Or maybe as the absence of interruption, inconvenience, and conflict, a stress-free security and complete contentment. We may think of peace as quiet, tranquility, freedom from disturbance, maybe even career success or financial security.

But so many of these things are out of reach. We can't always be successful or financially well off. Hardship comes. Confusion comes. Storms rise.

I don't know about you, but my times of being alone watching snow fall in the mountains or waves lap against the shore are infrequent. Okay, they are never. And in a family of many people—toddlers, preteens, teenagers, and adults—a calm and quiet atmosphere free of interruption basically does not exist. Your situation may be different, but I bet calm and quiet still feel elusive. Maybe your job or your studies are demanding, your financial situation continually uncertain, your relationships draining. You might be caring for an ailing loved one, striving to serve your community, longing to build relationships. Whatever the case, the absence of disturbance or inconvenience feels completely unachievable.

As much as we sometimes might want to, we can't just quit our lives, abdicate our responsibilities, and head to the beach or the bathtub.

I think our answer from Jesus would be that these things aren't really what we should be striving for anyway. Remember the disciples and all their hard work? Remember Jesus stopping to feed the five thousand? When I look at the life of Christ, I see just how often He *was* inconvenienced, interrupted, and right in the middle of a loud and chaotic atmosphere. Yet He Himself is the Prince of Peace, and He promises to leave this peace with us.

⌒

IN JOHN 13, Jesus the Messiah washes His disciples' feet and then, in the next chapter, gives them His longest recorded set of instructions. After sharing all sorts of directives and revelations, He looks at those He loves dearly, the ones who have left their lives and families to follow Him, and says, "Peace I leave with you; my peace I give you. I do not give to you as the world gives. Do not let your hearts be troubled and do not be afraid."[2]

In the very last hours of His life, knowing that He will soon face death, undeserved punishment, cruel torture, Jesus is concerned with His disciples' *hearts*. My mind and my body cannot be free from anxiety until I fix my heart on Him. "Do not let your hearts be troubled," Jesus says, and I confess: My heart is all too often troubled, and I know that yours is too.

"*My* peace I give you," Jesus tells His disciples. But look a bit earlier in the passage or at the verses right after and we see that Jesus is describing His impending death and warning His disciples of all manner of terrible things that are going to happen to them. He has warned them of their own sin and shortcomings and all the persecution and difficulty they are about to face. He says, "I have told you these things, so that in me you may have *peace*. In this world you will have trouble. But take heart! I have overcome the world."[3]

Take heart? John doesn't record the disciples' response here, but I know what mine would have been. Jesus has just told them that He is going to be betrayed and killed—that He is "going away."[4] They have given up their entire lives to follow Him, and He is going to leave? My reaction would have been to panic, but He instructs His disciples to grab hold of the opposite: deep peace and assurance.

Jesus isn't telling them to take heart because it will be easy. The disciples aren't looking forward to a moment of quiet or a beach vacation, the absence of chaos or trial or the perfect circumstances. They don't have success, financial freedom, or quiet lives to look forward to. They—we—are to take heart because Jesus, whose peace is not of this world, has overcome this world. There is no chaos or trial or circumstance that does not bow to Him. There is no hardship that we cannot trust Him with. "I am with you always," He says.[5] As our circumstances change, He does not. This is reason to rest. This is reason to rejoice. This is reason for peace.

We are thirsty for His peace, His deep rest, soul rest that remains true regardless of our circumstances. And we cannot find this peace in the world or in our outward circumstances. This peace can only be found in the person of Jesus Christ, the Prince of Peace, who meets

## THE PEACE JESUS GIVES

What does *peace* mean to you? What comes to mind when you think of that word? How does it contrast with this biblical definition of peace: deliverance, salvation, wholeness, completeness?

Peace isn't a feeling; it's a promise that finds fulfillment in a Person.

- In what ways have you been chasing the world's idea of peace instead of pursuing Jesus?
- What external circumstances have you blamed for your lack of peace?
- What have you imagined peace would look like, and how does knowing that Jesus Himself wants to be your peace change your expectations for today?

us in our turmoil, who is unchanged by the chaos of our world or the fluctuation of our emotions.

We find peace only in Jesus Himself because He is the only constant. He is the only one who doesn't change. He is the only one we can count on. Over and over in Scripture, Jesus offers people peace, blesses people with peace, and instructs them to "Go in peace."[6]

So we have this promise. Now what? How do we actually experience peace without just glossing over struggle and hardship with Christian platitudes?

Jesus points at our hearts: "Let not your hearts be troubled." So often, I am looking for peace in the *external*—my circumstance, my location, my life season, my absence of emergencies or interruptions —but the shift I need is *internal*. It is my heart that needs to be steadied, that needs to be changed.

I want a peace that permeates my life and flows out of it. I want a peace that settles down over my heart so that even as the world around me is pulled apart, my thoughts and emotions are fixed on a constant savior, a sure eternity, and a certainty that we are safe in His hands. I want to be able to breathe deeply and keep my bouncing knee and my fidgeting fingers still because I know that Jesus is in the boat with me, no matter the storm I am facing. *As I attune my heart to His, I can have a peace that transcends all circumstance, that overcomes the world.*

A study of the word *peace* Jesus uses in His final instructions to the disciples reveals the Old Testament Hebrew word *shalom*. While in a few cases this word could be used to mean "at rest" or "quiet," which is what comes to mind for me first when I think of peace, much more often it is used to mean "deliverance" or "salvation."

I spent some time letting that sink in after I first read Jesus's word to the disciples. When He says, "My peace I give you," He—our deliverance and salvation—is also saying, *I will be with you.* He is Immanuel, God with us. He is with us in the rapids. He is with us in the boat. Peace is ours because our deliverance and salvation come from Him. *He Himself is our peace.*

In Greek, this same word is translated *eiréné* and most often is assigned the meaning "complete" or "whole."[7] When Jesus gave peace to His disciples, to you and me, might He have been saying that He was making us whole and complete by inviting us into salvation and delivering us from sin and death? Whole and complete, *the very opposite of pulled apart and divided*? Was He offering an invitation to return to perfect fellowship with God, walking with Him as Adam and Eve had back when the world was the very definition of peace, shalom, a *complete* and *whole* universe? And if that is the case, what does it mean for how we live now, how we engage with a world that is so much less than whole, complete, and delivered, and how we look forward in salvation to the eternity that awaits us? Jesus says:

- *Do not let your hearts be troubled, because I am your peace.*
- *Do not let your hearts be troubled, because in Me, you are whole and complete.*
- *Do not let your hearts be troubled, because I have overcome.*
- *Do not let your hearts be troubled, because I am your salvation and deliverance and you are sealed for eternity with Me.*
- *Do not let your hearts be troubled, and do not be afraid, because no matter what comes, you are safe all along.*

All of Scripture is singing God's song of peace over us. My husband sings the words of Isaiah 43, and I often hum the tune to myself:

When you pass through the waters,
    I will be with you;
and when you pass through the rivers,
    they will not sweep over you.

When you walk through the fire,
> you will not be burned;
> the flames will not set you ablaze.
For I am the LORD your God,
> the Holy One of Israel, your Savior.[8]

Throughout all time, peace isn't just a suggestion from God; it is a command and a promise. As those who put our trust fully in Him, we are instructed not to be afraid and are promised that peace is possible.

"Because you are precious in my eyes," God continues, speaking through Isaiah, "and honored, and I love you."[9] *He will save us because He loves us.* He promises us peace because we are precious to Him. "Fear not, for I have redeemed you; I have called you by name, you are *mine.*"[10]

The peace that Christ longs to give us (and *has* given us in the Holy Spirit) is a confidence, a certainty, a quiet trust that we will be safe because of Him.

In the very beginning, in the garden, God wove peace into everything He created. He breathed over a void and chaotic mess and spoke life, beauty, and His perfect peace. It is the same peace that He will give us today if we respond to His command, not by somehow fixing our external circumstances but by turning our hearts toward Him.

We are promised that we can say confidently, like Abigail, in the face of any trial, "God who kept us safe before will keep us again." We are promised that even when the very foundations of the earth seem to be shaking, God will not remove His peace from us, because of His great love *for us.*

Jesus wants us to have the peace that Abigail has found, that many servants of God who have run this race before us have found.

He desires for us to live with hearts that are not troubled or fearful, but He adds a caveat: "I do not give to you as the world gives."[11]

We have been taught that peace is something we can make. I can take a sick day. I can run that bath and light a candle. Maybe if I could just turn the noise off for a few minutes I could find it! These things might help momentarily, but this peace doesn't last. The bath runs cold, the calendar fills up, and the noise comes right back.

The peace of the world is fleeting—interrupted by a screaming toddler, a conflict, a million different things that are outside our control. Jesus's peace, one that we are told transcends our human understanding,[12] is vastly different from the peace this world has to offer, or the illusion of it. Peace is a matter of the heart, not our external circumstances. Where the world leaves us divided, pulled apart, stretched in all different directions, Jesus offers deliverance, salvation, *wholeness*.

The peace that Jesus gives us doesn't go away when a crisis hits or the policies change or there is a natural disaster or our finances run out. When we have no control over our circumstances and no idea what is ahead, we can still know the peace of Christ that Jesus left with His disciples, the peace that Abigail has embraced.

⌒

A FEW MONTHS ago, I was able to connect with Abigail by Face-Time. Through the terribly spotty connection from our now being on different continents, she shared that cattle raiders had come and stolen her cows. I wept.

"Why are you crying?" she asked. "They are just cows. The Lord gave them to me, and He has now taken them. When He wants to, He will give us more."

"You are right," I conceded, "but I just worry about you there."

"Don't worry about us!" She laughed. "The Lord knows exactly when He will take each one of us. He says that nothing will ever separate us from His love, not even death. So if the cattle raiders come, whether we live or die, we will be with Him. That's enough."

*That's enough.* Abigail knows who she is because she knows *whose* she is.

I want to say that, and to believe deep in my bones that it's true. But I come from a place and a culture where we always reach for more, always look for better. Where accumulation and achievement are valued far more highly than God's presence and provision, even if we aren't willing to admit it. My worry for Abigail, for my own children, for other loved ones both in Uganda and in the United States, comes from the subtle thought in the back of my mind that God owes us something—safety, food, cows, health, life—and that if I try hard enough, work hard enough, pray hard enough, do well enough, I will be able to secure the life I want for us.

Abigail, the kindest, bravest, most faithful human being I know—surely she *deserves* better than having her cows stolen and her garden withering away in the drought again.

What if I got rid of that thinking? What if I truly believed that God owes me nothing at all (He doesn't) and that every single breath He gives, every provision I see around me, is a lavish gift to be thankful for? What if I accepted every hardship that comes my way, everything I view as lack of provision, as simply a bump in the road, remembering that nothing can separate me from His love for me and therefore no threatening crisis has any real power over my peace and security?[13]

I'll tell you a secret: We can't ditch anxiety by ourselves. Peace isn't something we can muster up from deep inside. Christ alone makes us whole, and Christ alone offers deliverance and salvation.

Jesus made a way for us to have this peace, wholeness, deliverance, salvation, when He went to the cross for us. Sinful man cannot have perfect peace with a righteous God, but because Jesus paid the price for our sin on the cross, He has made us whole, and God looks on us and sees the righteousness of His Son!

*He has already done everything needed to secure our perfect peace, our eternity with Him.* Because of His death on the cross and His glorious resurrection three days later, there will be a day when the whole earth, ourselves included, is made perfectly whole with no more sadness or suffering or fear or anxiety.

Abigail lives like this is true. The disciples (eventually) lived like this was true. Other followers of Christ through the centuries have looked not to the waves and rapids of this life to inform their peace but to Christ.

The life that God has planned for us likely won't be all still waters and calm quiet—"In this world you will have trouble"—but He will be with us in the waves, in the rapids, in the storms.

He will be our peace.

# 5

## CONTROL FREAK

The man said, "Let me go, for it is daybreak."

But Jacob replied, "I will not let you go unless you bless me."

—GENESIS 32:26

On a mundane Monday in the middle of our own family catastrophe and a worldwide pandemic, I sat down on the floor to play Candy Land with my son. Setting aside my work in the middle of the day is excruciatingly hard for me; there are always dishes to be done and laundry to be folded and something to be wiped down and usually at least a few people in need of my help and my attention. But I knew my five-year-old needed the connection and I did too, so I willed myself to still my racing thoughts, ignore my to-do lists, and play a board game with him.

When I got up to get a glass of water, I noticed him rearranging the cards to make sure that he got the ice-cream cone. In case you're unfamiliar with the rules of Candy Land, this card gets you the farthest ahead on the game board. He made sure I got the lollipop, which also moves you farther ahead but not as far as the ice-cream cone. He wanted to win but not by a landslide. He's sweet to me like that. He also ensured that no one got the peppermint card. Getting the peppermint is the worst. It basically takes you all the way back to the beginning. In fact, when my kids were younger, I used to just remove the peppermint altogether to spare us the sheer devastation (and tears) of having to go back to Peppermint Forest. If you know, you know.

I resumed my seat on the floor and played Candy Land with my little guy, pretending I had no idea that the cards were rearranged and acting surprised when he won by just a little bit. When we decided to play again, he asked me to get him some water while he "shuffled" the cards. I watched again as he carefully and thoughtfully arranged them. He was going to let me win this time. This went on for several games in a row, my son always asking me for something while he carefully arranged the cards to orchestrate the outcome that he wanted. As I watched him meticulously calculating every move, stacking the deck to make sure things would go as planned, he reminded me a little of myself.

*Control freak* is not a term I tend to use to describe myself. Externally, I appear to be more free-spirit hippie than type A organized. On the surface, I am just not the kind of person you would think was battling issues of control, shame, and anxiety. My house is always strewn with toys, and at least one unfolded laundry pile usually graces the couch, even when company is coming. We've hosted all kinds of things over the years—youth groups, homeschool co-ops, even our church—and I've learned the art of tidying up quickly and just enough that a space feels somewhat in order. We live in a little rural neighborhood, and I give my little ones free rein in the yard most days, shirts and shoes optional. We even show up to the store or school pickup regularly without any shoes. I guess the point I am trying to make here is that I am pretty low-key.

But as I watched my son rearranging his cards to ensure the perfect outcome, I realized that internally I maintain the narrative that I can be low-key because *I've got things all under control.* Until I don't. Until my loved ones are hurting and there's absolutely nothing I can do about it. Until there is no money in the bank and few opportunities to bring in more. Until the world is in disarray and nothing I can do will be even a drop in the bucket toward a solution. Until I am looking at the future and have no idea what is up ahead.

As I continued to ask the hard questions about the source of my panic and anxiety, as I reflected on the past many years of life and ministry, I was overwhelmed with just how much loss we had faced, how much pain I had just "pushed through," telling myself that it was for the sake of my children and those around me, hurrying toward the next thing instead of processing the deep losses and disappointments that often pummeled us like waves of the sea.

Pain and crisis had taught my brain and my heart to anticipate more pain and crisis, and without even realizing it, my thoughts were rushing away from today, into the future, trying to predict and then eliminate any hurt that might take me or my family by surprise again. *I wanted to stack the deck of cards myself.* I wanted to do everything I could right now to ensure the outcome I wanted, the outcome where we win, where none of my family members or friends face hardship or struggle or the devastation of having to start all over again.

My precious five-year-old had determined that in order to have a happy afternoon with me, he needed to win a game, let me win a game, and organize a game that was a tie. I had determined that in order for myself and my family to be okay, in order for my children to grow strong and healthy and love the Lord, in order for things to go well, *I needed to be in control.*

I had begun to trust my ever-fluctuating emotions over the Word of God. I had begun to believe in what I could see rather than the truths of God's promises that I could not see. I was trusting in my feelings and my own experiences over trusting in the security of my savior. My thoughts were racing ahead to try to control the future instead of living for today and trusting that my loving Father would take care of the future for me, for all of us.

No matter who you are, what season of life you are in, what your job or ministry or family looks like, I would be willing to bet that is true of you too.

Maybe you've felt compelled to keep a brave demeanor in front of your kids even while your heart was crushed by the death or illness of a parent. Maybe you returned to work as soon as possible after cancer surgery because you wanted to just feel normal. Maybe your marriage is falling apart but you just keep checking off your usual to-do list rather than acknowledging the pain even to yourself.

Or maybe you are grasping for control in some other ways, believing that if you could just get that new job or win the approval of that one person or move to that place, then everything would finally be okay and you could protect yourself and loved ones from the pain that just keeps coming.

I think most of us have internalized the idea that we can succeed, we can achieve, and we can produce on our own, and therein lies our security. But that thought is keeping us pulled apart, far from resting in the peace and wholeness our savior longs to give.

GENESIS 32 GIVES the well-known account of Jacob, grandson of Abraham, wrestling with God. It's important to note the circumstances that have led up to this moment. Jacob is part of the family line through which God will later send His Son, the Savior of the world.

As children, Jacob and his brother, Esau, were serious rivals, Esau the father's favorite and Jacob the mother's favorite. They are in constant competition. Even though God has already revealed to Jacob's parents, Isaac and Rebekah, that Jacob will inherit the family's birthright, it seems they forget along the way. Jacob, with the help of Rebekah, essentially tricks his father into giving him the family blessing when his father appears ready to ignore God's directive. Esau swears that he will kill Jacob for stealing what he believes to be his, and at the urging of his mother, Jacob runs away.[1] All four of them are seemingly just like my five-year-old and me—rearranging the cards to "ensure" a certain outcome, when in reality they are just making it harder for themselves to get to the place God was going to bring them anyway.

Because God remains a good and loving Father, Jacob is blessed even as he continues in his own patterns of sinning and then repenting and then sinning again. (Sound familiar?) Jacob travels to the places God shows Him. He marries and has many children. God gives him land and flocks, a big family, and great wealth. Jacob has all the marks of a very successful man in his day and age. And then God calls him to go back to the land he came from. And that means going back to where Esau, who swore to kill him, is still living.

It has been more than twenty years since Esau's threats, but Jacob is clearly worried. When messengers come to let Jacob know that Esau is coming to meet him with four hundred men, Jacob begins to panic.

"Great fear and distress" is how Genesis describes Jacob's state of mind, and understandably so. He calls out to God in desperation,

> O God of my father Abraham, God of my father Isaac, LORD, you who said to me, "Go back to your country and your relatives, and I will make you prosper," I am unworthy of all the kindness and faithfulness you have shown your servant. . . . Save me, I pray, from the hand of my brother Esau, for I am afraid.[2]

Jacob acknowledges who God is and what He has instructed him to do. He remembers God's past faithfulness and provision. But still, he is panicking. Even after he prays and asks God for protection,

## SURRENDERING CONTROL

I'd like to tell you that I've found a way to choose surrender without a struggle, but that isn't true. I am a lot like Paul, who says in Romans 7, "What I want to do I do not do, but what I hate I do."[8] Can you relate? Intellectually, I know that I am not in control, nor do I actually want to be in charge of everything. Experientially, I *know deeply* that God's plans are so much better than mine and that things go better when I stop trying to be in control and instead submit to Him.

So why is surrender this hard?

Part of it is because of how God made me. I am a strong woman with a strong personality; I have big goals and dreams, and I love to be able to influence others for Jesus and make a difference in the world around me. Another part of it is because of my sin nature: I will have to fight to trust God until the day He takes me to heaven to be with Him. Sanctification isn't a onetime thing; it's something we surrender to each and every day. Thankfully, He's not done with me yet, and the same is true for you.

Give some thought to the areas of life where you are most inclined to want to stack the deck in your favor. What are you trying to control? What are the hardest things to surrender to God, to truly trust Him with? Where do you fear His plans might be different from yours? Make a list of everything that keeps you awake or sends your thoughts spiraling into worry.

Now imagine yourself as Jacob, wrestling with God. When you stop struggling and simply look at His face, what do you see? How does looking at Him affect your perspective on facing whatever lies ahead?

even after he reminds himself of God's promises to him, Jacob makes frantic plans for how he might save himself from the wrath of his brother. He starts dividing his family members and animals into groups, thinking that if Esau begins to kill one group, the others might still be able to flee to safety. He carefully selects goats and camels and donkeys to present as gifts to Esau, probably hoping that he might pacify his brother's anger or buy his way into favor with these lavish presents.[3]

Just in case.

Sound familiar? *Princess Lollipop: check. Queen Frostine: check. Throw out Mr. Mint. Watch out for Lord Licorice.*

I confess that I do the same. I know what God has done for me and what He has promised me. I hope that I am quick to testify of His faithfulness and provision. I have seen His promises prove true again and again and again. I can look back on the most difficult periods of my life and see that He was good and He was kind and He was working, even when I didn't know or recognize it. I can say with Jacob that I am unworthy of the kindness and faithfulness that God has shown me time and time again.

I cry out to Him, ask Him desperately to protect and provide for me and my loved ones. I believe that He hears my prayers.

And then I make my best-laid plans . . . *just in case.*

Does Jacob actually trust God as he cries out to Him? His words say yes, but his actions seem to indicate otherwise. Just like Eve—just like *me*—Jacob wonders, *Will God really give me what I need? Are God's promises really true?*

Even after asking God for protection, Jacob lies awake. And I know this kind of night, lying sleepless in my bed, thoughts of "what if" and "if only" rolling through my head, dread and anxiety causing me to toss and turn as all my imagined worst-case scenarios loom larger and larger in the dark. I try to plot a way out of my predicament. I mentally retrace my steps, thinking how things might be different, might be better if only I had done that instead or if only I could tip this aspect of the situation just a little bit to my favor. I wrestle. Jacob wrestles.

In his case, quite literally. Having sent the others ahead, Jacob is alone that night when God appears, and the two grapple until daybreak, with Jacob refusing to let go until God gives him a blessing.[4]

Just like in the garden, God comes. God is after Jacob, just as He's always coming after us, always reaching for us, always meeting us. I don't know how to imagine Jacob wrestling with God. Is there a physical person, or is Jacob more like me, thrashing about in sleeplessness, wrestling with doubt and skepticism, wanting to believe that God will protect him but hearing the hiss of the serpent loud in his ear, saying, "What if He doesn't?"

Jacob has obeyed God, Jacob has done what He asked him to do in returning to his homeland, and now, well, what if He doesn't come through? Or what if letting Esau get revenge *is* part of the plan? What if sometimes, as we fear, God's plan really will take us through our worst nightmares and darkest valleys? What if we don't want to face what He might have up ahead? That thought alone is enough to make us feel like we are wrestling with a full-grown man.

Finally, God touches Jacob's hip socket in just the right place to overpower him. And as Jacob finally surrenders, *he sees the face of God.*

The man [God] asked him, "What is your name?"

"Jacob," he answered.

Then the man said, "Your name will no longer be Jacob, but Israel, because you have struggled with God and with humans and have overcome." . . .

Then he blessed him there.

So Jacob called the place Peniel, saying, "It is because I saw God face to face, and yet my life was spared."

The sun rose above him as he passed Peniel, and he was limping because of his hip.[5]

Jacob has known God's faithfulness, and he has known the disaster and consequence of taking things into his own hands. It sounds like the garden, doesn't it? It sounds like the Israelites, doesn't it? It is the story that all of human history is writing, this wrestling with God, us running and God coming, us hiding and God finding, us sinning and God restoring. He just keeps showing up in grace, even when that means He has to literally cripple Jacob to get him to stop fighting and just *look at His face.*

Surrender is where we see the face of God.

Surrender is where we know Him.

Surrender is where He shows us His beauty.

I WATCH MY son stack the deck and think briefly of how much beauty I would have missed if things had always gone according to my carefully laid plans. If none of my loved ones had ever walked in tragedy, we never would have gotten to rejoice in their restoration. If no one I loved was ever sick or hurting, we never would have gotten to celebrate their healing. If I hadn't spent so many sleepless nights calling out to the Lord, I wouldn't know the lines on His gentle face the way I do now, the way that feels comfortable and familiar, like when things get too hard I could just reach out and He would be right there. How would Jacob have seen the face of God if he hadn't wrestled? How would *I*?

I know this. But, of course, in the midst of anguish and uncertainty, such beauty seems unthinkable, unreachable. So like Jacob, I run right back to my old habits. I grasp at control. I believe that I will protect my family; I will ensure everything is in order; I will strive to make sure everyone is healthy and happy and well provided for. I lie awake making plans for crises that haven't happened yet. I have imaginary conversations over and over again in my mind. My desire for control yanks me away from the peace God offers and leaves my mind spinning in anxiety once more—pulled apart.

I sit back down on the floor and dutifully move my yellow plastic gingerbread man along the rainbow-colored trail of squares to the candy castle. I realize that my deep need to control didn't come from a longing for organization or an orderly life but from a rich, deep place of love for the people around me. I desperately desire for everyone—my friends, my family members, the children of Uganda, the homeless person on the corner—to *thrive*. And this is a good and noble pursuit. I desire to love and serve well my children, my loved ones, my neighbors, and the whole world. I want to take away all their pain and keep them from any future pain.

But I also begin to see that my God-given love for the people I care about the most, namely my family, has gradually warped into an idol, as I believed that thinking through every possible future scenario might somehow protect them from future pain. What had started as completely good and right—care and concern for my loved ones—had morphed into something ugly as I slowly began to believe the lie that somehow I was more equipped than our loving Father to control my future and theirs.

I know it's impossible. It seems ridiculous to even type out on my computer screen. But buried deep down beneath that love is the very same lie Adam and Eve believed in the garden—that maybe God isn't enough. *Maybe I can be the savior.*

Ugh.

When will I learn to surrender?

I want to; I intend to. I frequently tell God I've surrendered something to Him. But then I see myself reaching over from the passenger seat and trying to take the wheel right back out of Jesus's hand.

IN JACOB'S CASE, the ending of the story is a good one. After his night of wrestling, he limps toward the place he will finally meet his brother. He must have been feeling some new certainty after being with the Lord, because he goes on ahead of his wives and children and servants, which was not the original plan. The implication is clear: *Beholding the face of God is the antidote to our swirling anxiety. Beholding the face of God gives us the courage to confront what is up ahead, even when we don't know what it is.*

> Jacob lifted up his eyes and looked, and behold, Esau was coming. . . .
>
> [Jacob] went on before them, bowing himself to the ground seven times, until he came near to his brother.
>
> But Esau ran to meet him and embraced him and fell on his neck and kissed him, and they wept. And when Esau lifted up his eyes and saw the women and children, he said, "Who are these with you?" Jacob said, "The children whom God has graciously given your servant."[6]

When Esau refuses the lavish gifts of Jacob—because seeing his brother for the first time in years and meeting his family and his children is gift enough—Jacob insists that his offerings be accepted, saying, "To see your face is like seeing the face of God."[7]

To rest his eyes on the brother Jacob had imagined might hate him, might kill him, to feel the loving embrace of forgiveness—in all of it, he recognized the kindness, the gentleness, the mercy of God. Jacob had been safe all along.

And to be fair, let's consider if it had gone the other way: God might have ordained that the family strife would remain, that Esau really would seek revenge on Jacob. The Bible is full of family discord, and so is real life. God led Jacob straight into forgiveness, but He would have been just as present with him if the path led into deep suffering.

One of the most compelling truths I find in his story is that Jacob and Rebekah's scheming accomplished nothing. They could have saved themselves a lot of strife and argument if they had just trusted God to orchestrate and execute His plan to give Jacob the birthright blessing.

What if you and I could internalize that truth about the blessing God has promised us? If we are in Christ, we are all headed for eternity. We can rest in the promises of God here and now as we journey toward heaven, or we can keep grasping for control. The outcome remains the same, but the journey might be a whole lot more enjoyable if we surrendered our carefully stacked deck and simply rested in His provision and goodness.

As my therapist says when I lament about all my plans going up in flames, "The peace you get from trying to plan out the whole future and be in control of it is false peace anyway." She is right, of course. Any control I *think* I have is just an illusion. No matter how I plan, and no matter how certain I am about what the future holds, *I really don't know.* I never actually had control over any of it. My ongoing exercise in surrendering to God isn't for Him; it's for me.

We can lay aside our fretting, our worrying, our plotting and scheming and card rearranging, and behold the face of God. We can trust that if He leads us through dark valleys of suffering, He will be near, and we can trust that He has beauty in store for us that we can't even imagine. Our worry accomplishes *nothing.* I know and I can testify that God uses the suffering we couldn't stop or predict, the plan that doesn't go our way, to draw us close to Him and teach us of His character.

# 6

## TRUSTING THE FATHER'S TENDER LOVE

*While he was still a long way off, his father saw him and was filled with compassion for him.*

—LUKE 15:20

When we first moved to the United States, we landed in a city I'd never set foot in before, though it's not far from where I was born in Tennessee. *Nothing* was familiar. Not only did I have to relearn to drive on the right side of the road while sitting on the left side of the vehicle, but I had absolutely no idea how to get anywhere.

I'm really not sure how anyone successfully moved to a new place before the advent of Google Maps. For the first months that we lived here, I turned the navigation on every single time I got in the car and I followed it everywhere. Now, of course, I know how to get to many places that we frequent. I can find my way to the grocery store and the kids' school and the park. I can almost get to church without help. But I still turn on the map sometimes: partly out of habit, and partly because I really like to watch that blue line charting my course.

I've noticed I'm not the only one. The other night, I glanced over and saw that even though I had *my* map on, my teenage daughter had *hers* on too, showing her the route and letting her know, to the minute, how much longer we would be in the car. When I asked her why, she said, "I just like to know, you know?"

Even our five-year-old loves to listen from his car seat in the back to the directions Siri calls out. He actually asks me to turn the sound up, despite it interrupting the podcast we are listening to. "Hey! I can't see the map!" he will yell when I have the phone turned slightly too far toward me.

*We all want to know where we are going.*

PROVERBS 3 WAS one of the first scriptures I ever memorized. Verses 5 and 6 were written on a painting in the laundry room of the home we moved into when I was in first grade. I liked the way they sounded, so I repeated them to myself until they stuck.

> Trust in the LORD with all your heart
>> and lean not on your own understanding;
> in all your ways submit to him,
>> and he will make your paths straight.

As a child, I loved the image those words painted: If I loved and trusted God, He would show me where to go, show me the path. What I am learning as an adult, though, is that His making my paths straight doesn't necessarily mean He's going to show me the path. It means that *He knows the path* and is going to make sure I get to the end of it. He doesn't give us a little blue line, because He gives us the opportunity to trust Him.

Chances are, if you grew up going to Sunday school, you know these verses too. It's easy for me to spout them from memory, but when I recently meditated on this passage, I realized just how much is packed into these few words.

First of all, what does it mean to trust God with *all* my heart? I have gotten very good at trusting Him with *some* things in my life, with some of my heart, with some of my hard. But the things that feel the hardest and the messiest are often the things I grip most tightly. The things I love the most—my children, my family, my home—are often the things I find hardest to trust Him with.

As the proverb goes on, God instructs us not to be wise in our own eyes, not to rely on our own understanding, and I realize that is exactly what all my managing and hustling and scheduling is, whether or not I want to admit it. When I seek to control a circumstance or an outcome, I am relying on *my* understanding, on what *I* can see, which of course, we know, is only a really small part of the picture.

As I contemplated these simple verses, I heard God calling me to Himself. To trust Him. To honor Him. *Only after I fully trust a good and loving God will I be able to surrender the thoughts and fears that are pulling me apart.* I could learn to trust Him more. I could learn to surrender. And He was promising that as I did, I would find the very life and peace I was looking for.

Several months after our family moved to the States, as I was spending time in prayer, I found myself saying over and over again, "Lord, I just can't see." As someone who has frequently been filled with vision about what life can and should look like, what's next, or what I feel God is calling me or my family toward, sitting in a season where I honestly had no clue what was up ahead felt totally terrifying. "I just can't see it, God," I cried. "I don't know what You want me to do."

We had felt affirmed in our decision to stay in the United States. God had opened countless doors in ways that could only be Him. And now here we were, gazing into a completely unknown, unfamiliar, uncomfortable future. I had no vision or hopes or dreams for what this next season of life could be like. The future seemed absolutely *blank*. And I found that not in the least exciting but instead terrifying.

As I sat and prayed and worshipped, these words dropped into my heart: *Fix your eyes on Me.*

I was straining to see into the future (a power I don't have and never will, by the way), straining to see the way through. I didn't just want Him to make my paths straight; I wanted Google Maps, that little blue line telling me exactly what was up ahead. I wanted Him to *make the path known to me.* Instead, God was asking me to look at His face, to trust that as I fixed my gaze on Jesus, He would direct my steps. Once again, my peace would begin on the inside, not by knowing, understanding, or even enjoying my external circumstance but by turning my heart toward Him.

Are you, like I am, feeling anxious about the path God is leading you on? Are you perhaps straining to anticipate what lies ahead, searching for an alternate route with fewer potholes and detours? Does the very idea of entrusting it all to God leave you feeling shaky? I understand.

In order to willingly surrender, you and I have to first look at His face and truly know who He is. We have to be confident that as we let go of our fears, our plans, our loved ones, we aren't just releasing them into nothing. We can be sure we are placing them into the safe, strong hands of a kind and loving God.

$\sim$

ONE OF MY favorite stories Jesus told is in Luke 15, commonly called the parable of the prodigal son. This young man knows what he wants and he goes after it. "Father," he says to his dad, "give me my share of the estate."[1] This is a bold ask, presumptuous and selfish, essentially the cultural equivalent of saying he wishes his father were dead. He wants his inheritance *now*. He wants to be in control of his destiny.

And surprisingly, the father complies. He gives the son his share of the money, and the son sets out to pursue the lavish lifestyle of his dreams, recklessly squandering the wealth he has been given. As is usually the case when we try to stack the deck in our favor, things go well for a while and then begin to unravel. A famine arose and the son found himself far away from home, out of money, out of luck.

I helped our children put on a play of this story one year for our community. I remember how much we all laughed during the scene when the son, who eventually gets work as a hired hand, becomes so desperate that he starts eating out of the same feeding trough as the pigs he is caring for. It's a funny picture, especially when cute toddlers are dressed up as the pigs. But it's a startling one too. When we try to run the world, this is how we end up: desperate, exhausted, destitute. Suddenly we wish we hadn't put ourselves in the position of control after all.

Just like Adam and Eve in the garden, just like Jacob with his injured hip, the son has his weakness exposed. He realizes that even the servants and hired hands in his father's household are living much better than he is now. "How many of my father's hired servants have food to spare, and here I am starving to death!" he ponders. "I will set out and go back to my father and say to him: Father, I have sinned against heaven and against you. I am no longer worthy to be called your son; make me like one of your hired servants."[2]

Talk about desperation. Talk about embarrassment. And I know the feeling. I can think of more than one time when I tried to take control of a situation against the wise counsel of my parents or, more recently, my husband, more than one time when I tried to run ahead of my Father God instead of waiting on Him to reveal His plans for me, and every time ended in embarrassment. I have said with the psalmist, "My guilt has overwhelmed me like a burden too heavy to bear."[3]

I remember talking with my children about how the son must feel as he trudges back home to face his father, the father he has been so rude to. *Certainly, my father won't want to see me. Certainly, he'll be angry. He'll probably yell and scream or, worse, give me the silent treatment. He probably won't even want to look at me.* These are the thoughts I imagine running through the son's mind as he walks the winding road home, head down in shame.

This is what *I* would be thinking anyway. I'm quick to chide myself, especially when I feel that I have failed. Especially when I know that I haven't waited on God or other voices of wisdom in my life and have forged ahead on my own without direction because I just wanted to do things my way, on my timeline. And when I realize that again, like Paul, I have done what I do not want to do and I have not done what I longed to do,[4] I become the person I imagine the son to be in this story: full of shame for my failure to surrender, scolding myself, imagining that my loved ones and even my heavenly Father are wildly disappointed in me. I hang my head and trudge home.

But if you can relate, there is good news for us. This part of the story leaves me speechless every time: "While [the son] was still a long way off, his father saw him."[5]

And to see someone from a long way off, you have to be looking for him. The father is waiting, looking for his son. *When we lose our way, our Father is waiting, looking for us.*

"His father . . . felt compassion, and ran and embraced him and kissed him."[6]

God isn't going to *make* us surrender. When we grab at control or race ahead without His guidance instead of trusting that He actually has a plan, and when we wallow in guilt and shame over all we have done wrong and run to hide, *our loving Father still adores us.* Our loving Father has compassion on us. Just like in the garden, He looks for us. He longs for us. And when we turn toward Him, He is ready and willing to embrace us!

What a relief. What a joy!

And just as Scripture promises, His kindness is intended to lead us to repentance.[7] The son falls to his knees and says, "Father, I have sinned against heaven and against you. I am no longer worthy to be called your son." And instead of agreeing with him, instead of scolding him, instead of berating him and telling him "I told you so," the father throws a party.

> The father said to his servants, "Bring quickly the best robe, and put it on him, and put a ring on his hand, and shoes on his feet. And bring the fattened calf and kill it, and let us eat and celebrate. For this my son was dead, and is alive again; he was lost, and is found." And they began to celebrate.[8]

The son's confession is true of us too. We *have* sinned against the Father, often more than we care to admit, and on our own, we *are* unworthy to be called His sons and daughters. Yet forgiveness is freely offered to us from our gracious Father because Jesus, who is infinitely worthy, took our place, and when God looks on us, He sees the worth of His Son. We are utterly beloved.

Oh, friend, our Father is so much kinder than we even dare to imagine. Just like in the garden, He is calling to you: "Where are you? Come home to me."

⁓

I REMEMBER THE way my newborn son looked up at me as the midwife placed him fresh and slimy on my chest. How he didn't really cry at first but just blinked, his little baby-gray eyes locked on mine. He looked at me and I looked at him. Right from the start, we adored each other.

Psychologists say that from the moment we're born, we long for someone to notice us, to see us, to meet our needs. Our babies are born looking for their parents. In the first year of life, an infant cries thousands of times, and thousands of times is picked up, rocked, changed, fed, reassured, crooned over. For a thousand cries, there are a thousand responses. The infant is looking for a caregiver, and a caregiver is seeing the infant's need and meeting it. This cycle happens over and over again, and eventually the baby learns they're *safe.*

Any adoptive parent knows that the most important thing when you bring a baby or child into your home is *attachment, attachment, attachment.* We work toward attachment with our kids above all else. Of course, a biological parent works at this too; it just comes a little more naturally sometimes.

When a child endures the terrible trauma of being separated from a birth parent or caregiver for any reason, attachment is broken, and it can be a long and arduous process to help them learn to attach to another adult. To help them learn to *trust.* One of the first things we are taught to do as foster or adoptive parents is get down on a child's level and look them in the eye. A child needs to know they are seen and loved and protected by someone who will take care of them.

It doesn't end in early childhood either. My teenage daughter lines up at the track starting block, and before her head bends to focus completely on the start, her eyes scan the crowd until they rest on mine. I'm here. I'm watching. She grins.

On another day, I sit in the audience of a school play and watch our middle schooler crane her neck from the back row of the chorus and exhale relief as she finds our motley crew right there in the middle row, ready to behold her performance.

My toddler runs to play in the sandpit at the park, but even as he digs, he occasionally peeks his head up just to make sure I am still there, still watching. *And we need the same assurance.* We are all longing to be noticed. To be seen. To be cared for. *To be precious to someone.* If only we would let our eyes find His gaze. In Matthew 6, part of Jesus's famous Sermon on the Mount, in urging His followers not to be anxious, He says,

> I tell you, do not worry about your life, what you will eat or drink; or about your body, what you will wear. . . . Look at the birds of the air; they do not sow or reap or store away in barns, and yet your heavenly Father feeds them. Are you not much more valuable than they? Can any one of you by worrying add a single hour to your life?
>
> And why do you worry about clothes? See how the flowers of the field grow. They do not labor or spin. Yet I tell you that not even Solomon in all his splendor was dressed like one of these. If that is how God clothes the grass of the field, which is here today and tomorrow is thrown into the fire, will he not much more clothe you—you of little faith?[9]

This is one of the most often quoted passages of Scripture when it comes to dealing with anxiety. I've even heard it said that "Do not be anxious about anything" is a command of Jesus. It certainly is. But if we stop after the first verse—"Do not worry [or be anxious] about your life"—and take just the command by itself, we can feel pretty discouraged. If you've ever dealt with anxiety, you know as well as I do that you can't just turn it off.

*I would quit being anxious if I could, trust me,* I used to think whenever I read this verse. I don't *want* to be anxious.

But Jesus isn't just commanding us to stop being anxious; He's

## HANDS OPEN, PALMS UP

Friend, look back at the list you made at the end of chapter 5. Over what areas of your life are you struggling to maintain control? Your financial security, the health and well-being of your children or parents, the happiness of your friends and family, your future?

What would it look like today to surrender these things to God? Can you imagine Him as the father of the prodigal son? Can you confess to Him that you've been trying to do it all on your own and then believe that He doesn't run from you but toward you in your mess? What if today you finally unclenched your fists and said to God, *I just can't do this anymore*? (Spoiler alert: He already knows that.)

I've started beginning my mornings with my hands open and my palms up, the way I often turn them during a powerful moment of worship. I invite you to join me in this posture as we offer up prayers of surrender. Mine are often as simple as "I give [person, situation, worry, fear] to You, Lord. I give You control." And I continue to whisper that until a particular anxiety is no longer swirling in my mind.

Of course, other things will crop up. You will notice, like I do, when you are trying to steal back from God things that you have already given Him control over. This isn't failure; it's human. Don't run and hide *from* God; run *to* Him. The important thing is that we learn to recognize when we are slipping back into our white-knuckle patterns of control and choose instead to loosen our grip, turning our palms skyward and saying, "It's all Yours, Lord. I believe! Help my unbelief."[18]

calling us to replace our anxiety with something else, something better. "Look," He says. *Look at the birds. Look at the flowers of the field.* And then He goes on to say, "Seek first the kingdom of God."[10]

*Look for Me,* He says. *Look to Me. Fix your eyes on Me.*

I've come to realize that when we surrender anything—such as our worry, our anxiety, or our desire for control—it leaves a hole, and that hole has to be filled with something or we will just pick the worry right back up again. So Jesus tells us to look to Him, look at Him, marvel at Him, stand in awe of Him. We fill the hole with Jesus. When we look at Jesus and realize that He is lovingly, kindly looking back at us, *our understanding of His love begins to fill the space that was consumed by our anxiety.* I have found that I cannot marvel at how loved and provided for I am by my Father and simultaneously panic about my future. I can surrender my worries to Him because I trust Him.

When Jesus instructed His disciples to believe in Him before He went to the cross,[11] that word for "belief" literally translates to *trust.* We can't just believe in Him; we must trust Him. Isaiah 26:3 says, "You will keep in perfect peace those whose minds are steadfast, because they trust in you." We will have peace only if our minds are steadfast, eyes fixed on the Savior, and we can be steadfast only when we trust Him, *because* we trust Him.

When we can't see what is up ahead and *merimna* anxiety is pulling us apart, we can fix our eyes on Jesus and begin to experience shalom, the *eiréné* peace that puts us back together and makes us whole. Because the God you are looking for is looking for you. Looking at you. Loving you.

⌒

ON OUR HONEYMOON, my husband and I sat on a hill in Israel similar to the one where Jesus probably gave the Sermon on the

Mount. It was amazing to witness the red, yellow, and purple wild-flowers springing up all over the hillside. Birds flew and chirped overhead. The breeze blew gently off the Sea of Galilee. There on the hill, it was easy to imagine what Jesus had been talking about. The flowers in all their splendor, the birds singing and carefree, all crafted and precisely provided for by their creator. If He has indeed clothed and provided for the flowers and the birds, how much more will He provide for us, His beloved, chosen people? *How much more will He clothe you?*

I remembered how He clothed Adam and Eve in the garden. After they had disobeyed the one rule God had given them, after they had run away in shame, the loving Father showed up and clothed them, provided for them.[12] And I sat there on the hill and thought of all the many, many times He has provided for me and my family, the times we have thought there would be no way and some-how He made one, the times we have thought we wouldn't have what we needed but somehow we did.

Jesus doesn't just instruct His followers not to be anxious; He re-minds them to trust in the Father, whose love is beyond measure. Jesus knows how easy it is to find our security in our circumstances: our food or finances, our clothing or housing, our job security or future plans. But we have to shift our eyes to look at Jesus, the One who ultimately will provide for all our needs, the One who is looking for us, loving us, valuing us above all else He created.

The writer of Hebrews instructs us to fix our eyes on Jesus, the author and perfecter of our faith.[13] When my anxiety cries out, *I just can't see what is up ahead,* the God of Peace beckons, "Look at Me. Eyes on Me, beloved."

What if we believed that He cares for us infinitely more than the flowers that grow free, the birds that are well fed without any work or toil? What if we could learn to fix our eyes on Him when we cannot see what is up ahead?

Remember in Mark 6, where Jesus got into the boat with the disciples amid the storm and calmed the waves?[14] There's a similar story in Matthew 14, or perhaps it's the same scene retold from a different perspective. In any case, the waves and the wind are crashing against the small boat, and the disciples are terribly afraid, when they see Jesus walking toward them on the water. As Jesus draws near the boat and tells them who He is, Peter calls out to Jesus, "Lord, if it's you . . . tell me to come to you on the water."[15]

"Come," Jesus says.

Then Peter gets down out of the boat, walks on the water, and goes to Jesus, but when he sees the wind, he is afraid and calls out, "Lord, save me!"[16]

I identify so much with Peter, one minute full of zeal and faith, the next minute shaky and uncertain.

There were times of my life when I trusted God unequivocally, with all my heart. When I leaned hard on Him even when I didn't understand my outward circumstances. Never have I known a deeper peace than when He invited me into something that seemed as impossible as walking on water and I gave Him my full, surrendered yes. When I moved to Uganda, when I began the process of adopting our girls, when I stepped into marriage with the man I love, when I opened our home to the sick and the dying. But so often, I find myself back in my control-and-anxiety cycle, crying out, *Lord, save me!*

Picture the tenderness in the eyes of the father as he welcomed home his prodigal son. I see this tenderness in Jesus after He reaches out to save Peter as they climb into the boat together.

"Why did you doubt?"[17] Jesus asks him—asks me—gently. *Why do I doubt Him?*

And here is what I wonder: Does God allow the rapids to help us learn to trust Him more? Not as a test but because He wants us to draw near to Him, wants us to know Him so intimately that He provides us with repeated opportunities to reach out for His hand and have Him rescue us? And does He graciously *not* allow us to see what is up ahead because then we would miss out on fixing our eyes on Him, looking at our God, who looks back at us with eyes full of love?

Jesus invites Peter to join Him on the water in the middle of the storm. When Peter can't rally the trust on his own to get to Jesus, Jesus gives it to him. When Peter falters, Jesus reaches out His hand. When we step into the waves and our thoughts begin to spiral, our control tendencies or shame or regret pulling us under, a God with love in His eyes waits there to receive us, stands reaching for us. Despite our faithlessness and our failings, He remains faithful. He will rescue us, His hand reaching out, our invitation to trust.

# 7

## OUR STORYTELLING GOD

*This is my beloved Son, with whom I am well pleased.*

—MATTHEW 3:17, ESV

Surrender, in its truest form, comes when we finally see ourselves as the runaway son did: broken, out of control, desperate, in need of rescue. And in my life, this isn't a onetime thing. Some of us may have been taught that we surrender our lives to God once, at the moment of salvation. But I have to surrender to Him continually, acknowledging my sin before Him like the prodigal son, returning to Him even when I have fallen short, trusting that He will still receive me lovingly and has my very best in mind. How often have I said, *Okay, God, I surrender; I give You control,* only to try to steal it back from Him a few days, weeks, or months later?

Today is a good example, actually. I began writing this chapter a few days ago feeling confident that I had made some great progress in trusting God and was finally truly living in a place of peace, trust, and surrender. But I got a hard phone call last night, and here I am again, tempted to panic, tempted to despair—and for what seems like good reason. One of the people I love most in the whole world is facing an obstacle that, barring a miracle, is insurmountable. It's not my story to tell, and today the details feel too heavy to reveal anyway. But I'll just tell you this: The situation looks bleak.

I've thought through all the potential outcomes, and none of them seem good. From my spot in the river, it really looks like maybe no fishermen will come to the rescue this time. Maybe God is going to allow my loved one to be pulled into the rapids. This might be really, really hard.

But I am reminded that there is no situation beyond His reach, no path too dark for His redemption to shine through.

We may never know the reason for suffering. But we will know that God is with us in it and that His presence will be infinitely better than understanding in the first place.

I believe all this and yet—

Once again I've got the "good" plan all mapped out in my head. *If only this would happen and then that would happen and then this would happen, this exact sequence at this exact time—well, then it will all be fine.* Once again I've let God know how *I* think things should go down. As I become aware once more that I am not actually in charge, my mind and my heart spiral. *Are You really going to ask me to surrender this, Lord?*

This is forever my struggle, and all of ours, I think: one minute saying, "I trust You, Lord. I do trust that You love me and You love my loved ones and You have a good, good plan for us even when we can't see it," and the next minute calling out, "Help! I'm drowning! How could You leave me here like this, God? And, God? This plan is a *mess!*" I identify with the sick boy's father in the Gospel of Mark who says to Jesus, "I do believe; help me overcome my unbelief!"[1] And the same way Jesus looked tenderly at that man as he asked for help, the same way the father mercifully embraced the prodigal son who had come home, my heavenly Father looks at me and says, *It's okay. Come to Me.* As I struggle and doubt and wrestle, I don't have to run and hide. In fact, I can go with this wavering right up next to my kind Father and rest my head on His chest.

In the pages to come, we'll talk about all sorts of practical ways to pursue peace, but first we need to know that no matter what systems we put in place and no matter how much of our calendars we clear or what rhythms of rest we institute, our real peace comes from knowing, believing, trusting that God is good and kind and absolutely in control, worthy of our worship and our utmost trust. This certainty calms not only our anxious thoughts about present challenges and an uncertain future but also our mental turmoil over past regrets.

THROUGHOUT MY YEARS of parenting adopted children and working with kids who have come from hard places and experienced unspeakable traumas in their early lives, I have read any and all material I can get my hands on about attachment and felt safety. I am fascinated by the ways our brains grow, change, and heal and by how the human brain can come up with all sorts of narratives for our past and our present that may not in fact be true but are rather a result of deep pain. Some of these narratives enable survivors of trauma to live through terrible and terrifying events. Some of these stories are the result of deep guilt and shame, even about things the child may have had no control over. These narratives can sound like this:

- *I will never be safe.*
- *I will never be loved.*
- *I can't trust anyone but myself.*
- *I will never have a place to belong.*
- *I am not safe here or anywhere.*

This inner turmoil, though it isn't the child's fault, is certainly the opposite of the peace that we long for, the peace God longs to give us. It takes a lot of intentionality and work, often trained professionals and even medication, to rewire the brain so it can receive rest, peace, and safety.

It took me years to realize that adults and children who have survived trauma or lived through unspeakable situations aren't the only ones operating under inaccurate narratives. I do this too. *We all do.*

We live in a world that constantly pressures us to tell a story, usually a false one. We head to social media to see others' lives perfectly manicured, happy, successful, and carefree. We are taught that we need to project the same. We find the perfect angle for the perfect picture so we can let the world know that our home is in order and our children are perfect and that we go to fun places and do fun things. We stop actually experiencing the lives right in front of us and instead watch them through our phone screens so that we can let everyone know just how great our lives are.

We are taught that to earn approval, we must spin a false narrative, a narrative that says that all is well and we are awesome and we are okay, even when we are not. We buy the world's lie that we must have it all under control, as we were already bent to want control anyway.

Deep in our thoughts and our hearts, though, many of us are telling ourselves other equally false narratives, completely opposite the ones we project to the world. After several years of good therapy, I have begun to realize that I am often telling myself a story that isn't really true.

As I think, pray, and, to be honest, worry about my children, these thoughts creep in:

- *I haven't done enough for them.*
- *I haven't prepared them well for the future.*

- *I've messed up their view of God.*
- *I should have disciplined less.*
- *I should have taught them more.*
- *I should have spent more one-on-one time with each of them.*
- *Maybe I didn't do any of this right.*
- *I am a terrible mother.*
- *I have failed them.*

As I consider my job and my ministry, these thoughts often appear:

- *I'm not really adding any value here.*
- *They don't need me.*
- *I have nothing to contribute.*
- *I am easily replaceable.*
- *None of my work matters.*
- *Maybe this was all for nothing.*

And as I think, pray, and sometimes worry about life in general, my thoughts sound a whole lot like the children from difficult situations whom I have worked with:

- *I am not lovable.*
- *I do not belong.*
- *I can't trust anyone but myself.*
- *I need to take control here.*
- *I am alone.*
- *I am not safe.*

And I have sat in circles of women in all different parts of the world and heard them saying these exact same things. Where did all this chastisement come from? If we go back to the picture of God who went to Adam and Eve in the garden, and the tender father of the prodigal son, we can be sure it didn't come from Him. But I grew up thinking (and many of my "good Christian" friends and community members affirmed it) that I had to do certain things and succeed at certain things and achieve certain things to be in the Good Christian Club so I could be counted among those beloved of God. And I didn't take this challenge lightly.

Now, of course, if I say any one of the things in the lists above to one of my close friends who really know me well, they are quick to say, "That isn't true." And when I pause and think from a place of trusting God and His Word instead of from a place of emotion, I *know* these thoughts aren't true. But that doesn't keep the serpent's lying hiss from sounding true, especially in the hard moments, on the lonely days, in the middle of the night.

And if I am not careful, I begin to believe this story I have concocted. I am Adam and Eve, hiding from God, certain that He will kill me when He finds out my sin. I am the prodigal son, imagining all the ways the father will berate me when I finally show up and admit my mistakes. I am Peter on the water, certain I will go under and drown.

As I have begun to vulnerably share these things, I've been overwhelmed to realize how many of the people I speak with have similar thoughts—especially amazing, strong, competent women! I suspect that in the lists above, you heard echoes of a few of the stories you've been telling yourself.

So many of us are carrying around guilt and shame, despite the truth that Christ has set us free! So many of us are telling ourselves stories of how terrible we are, how dangerous life is, and how badly we have failed. Simultaneously, many of us are trying to tell the world the story of how great we are, how great our life is, how everything is okay. *How we've got it all under control.* No wonder we feel as if we're constantly being pulled apart!

Guess what? Both of these ways of presenting ourselves are in contradiction to the story God is telling us and the story He tells about us.

In Matthew 3:17, long before Jesus calms any storms or performs any signs or wonders, God proclaims His pleasure in His Son: "This is my beloved Son, with whom I am well pleased." And when we repent of our sin and put our full hope in Jesus, *these words become true of us too.*[2] We are His beloved, with whom He is well pleased.

Take a moment to put this book down and breathe that in. Wherever you are, close your eyes and spend a moment in silence, allowing His voice to rise up from your heart. He is assuring you, *You are My beloved child, and I am well pleased with you.* Can you receive it? Can you believe it? We can cease our striving because of Christ.

Before eating of the fruit, Adam and Eve stood naked and they were not ashamed. Because of Jesus, we can go to our heavenly Father like that now. Do we believe it? Do we believe that He looks on us tenderly, as individuals precious to Him, with a love for us and a desire to provide for us and protect us? We are His precious children, and it is His delight to pour out His peace on our lives!

As someone who is self-critical by nature, I often find it difficult to believe that God adores me unconditionally, regardless of my performance, my struggles, and my sin. I constantly have to remind myself that I can't earn His love or approval—I already have it. *How could He truly be well pleased with me after I have failed again?* I chide myself. Because of Jesus, who fulfilled all righteousness. Because of Jesus, who took my place.

I mentioned in the previous chapter how my children often look for me at track meets and sporting events, at school performances and graduations, venturing off to play but always glancing back over their shoulders to make sure I'm watching. They aren't the only ones who grin when our eyes meet. I delight in knowing that they have seen me watching them. I pray that all throughout their lives, as they scan their surroundings for me, they are met with a gaze that is delighted, not in what they are doing but in who they are and in the fact that they are mine.

And if this is true of me, an undeniably *imperfect* parent, how much more is this true of God, the perfect Father? The psalmist says that God rescued him because He delighted in him. The prophet Zephaniah says that God takes great delight in us and rejoices over us![3]

Oh, friend, the God we are looking for is gazing back at us with great love, great delight in His eyes. No matter how loudly the false narratives protest, we are His beloved, in whom He is well pleased.

Before we dive in further, list some areas of your life where you are having trouble believing that God adores you. What do you need to bring to Him naked and unashamed? Maybe it is a dream or a plan, a sin, a struggle, a past mistake. Imagine laying whatever it is down at His feet. Imagine His eyes on you, loving you, His precious son or daughter.

Now read aloud the words of Paul in Romans 8:

There is now no condemnation for those who are in Christ Jesus. . . .

And we know that in all things God works for the good of those who love him, who have been called according to his purpose. . . .

If God is for us, who can be against us? He who did not spare his own Son, but gave him up for us all—how will he not also, along with him, graciously give us all things? Who will bring any charge against those whom God has chosen? . . . Who will separate us from the love of Christ? . . .

In all these things we are more than conquerors through him who loved us.[4]

We are loved. We are safe. We can trust Him. This is the *true* story. But if it feels hard to believe, trust me, I understand.

A FEW YEARS ago, I was criticized quite publicly for my adoptions, my ministry, my parenting, basically my entire adult life. At first I

## REWRITING THE NARRATIVE

If you find yourself often stuck and spiraling in an untrue narrative or plagued with guilt and shame, I want to offer you a couple suggestions that are helping me slowly climb out of this place.

### SEEK OUT TRUTH TELLERS

Gather some people who know you really well, who have lived the story with you. Share with them vulnerably the guilt or shame you are carrying. Likely, they remember the story a little differently.

When I was being publicly bashed for basically every important decision of my life and beginning to believe some of the lies, a few close friends came around me to tell me the truth. "That's not how it happened," they assured me. "We were there." I could believe them even when I couldn't hear the voice of God and couldn't trust my own voice.

We are all going to have moments of wondering, *Am I doing this right? Am I contributing anything? Have I messed this all up?* Grab your trusted people and pull them in close. When I did, I tried not to let it get to me, but as more and more people chimed in online, saying terrible, untrue things about me for the whole world to read, it was hard to keep perspective. I will be the first to admit that I have made mistakes, *countless mistakes,* in parenting, in ministry, and in every other area of my life. I am hard on myself, and I don't usually need to be reminded that I fall short. To have my shortcomings magnified, taken out of context, and thrown about flip-

had a handful of amazing friends who were able to look me in the eye and say, "You didn't mess it all up. I saw you. I saw you giving it your all. I saw you doing your best. I saw you being a good mom. *I was there.*"

## IMMERSE YOURSELF IN GOD'S TRUTH

Dig into the Word of God. It's the only absolute truth that we have. It is our true story in a world that is telling us all sorts of lies and when we are telling ourselves a false narrative as well.

When you can't hear God's voice or He seems distant, begin to list the things that you know are true of Him and that you know He says are true of you. Let's get started together:

- God is always good, kind, and merciful.[11]
- God is always for you.[12]
- God has a plan, a *good* plan.[13]
- God is sovereign, or, in simpler terms, in complete control.[14]
- You are cherished.[15]
- You are created in the image of Holy God.[16]
- You are chosen by God.[17]
- You were created for a purpose.[18]
- You are victorious over your circumstances in Christ.[19]

pantly on a public platform was deeply wounding to me. More than that, I began to lose sight of what was actually true.

I hope and pray you never face criticism in a public sphere like this. But we all face some sort of criticism, some sort of disapproval from others and the internal disapproval of ourselves. Sometimes a lie is close enough to the truth that we start to believe it. Remember how the Enemy whispered, "Didn't God say you can't eat from *any* tree?" That wasn't really what God said, but it was close enough to the truth to be believable.

Being misunderstood and misrepresented is deeply painful, and if we let them, those untruths can become so loud that they weave themselves into the story we are telling ourselves and eventually become a story we believe. Repeat the story to ourselves often enough and we might find ourselves naked and hiding in the bushes in shame, running from our kind and gracious Father, with no real idea of how we got there.

I once heard psychiatrist Curt Thompson say that it takes our brains less than three seconds to encode a memory of shame and sixty to ninety seconds to encode a memory of joy.[5] As devastating as that statistic is, I felt so relieved to hear it. There wasn't something wrong with me. It wasn't unique to me that shame had been so hard to shake. It was deeply encoded into my brain.

If you are feeling deep shame, guilt, or regret over past mistakes, please know this: God can redeem all our mistakes. The biggest ones, the darkest ones, the deepest ones. We don't have to run and hide from a God who longs to clothe us in mercy and salvation.[6]

I am deeply encouraged by the life and faith of the apostle Paul, also known as Saul. Before an encounter with the risen Jesus totally changed his life, Paul was a Pharisee. He was revered for following the Jewish law and, more importantly, for *persecuting* followers of Jesus. He prided himself on going to great lengths to torture and even murder those who followed Christ.

And then one day, as he was on his way to torture more Christ followers, a light from heaven flashed around him and a voice called his name: "Saul, Saul, why do you persecute me?"[7] Understandably afraid, Paul fell to the ground and asked where the voice was coming from.

Jesus answered, "I am Jesus, whom you are persecuting."[8] We don't get a ton of detail about the rest of Paul's encounter with Jesus, but we know that he was blind and alone for three days and that Christ revealed the whole Gospel to him in their time together.[9] Paul went on to become a minister of the Gospel all over what is now Europe and the Middle East. Paul faced terrible persecution and near death again and again, yet during that time he was able to write many books of the New Testament.

What did Jesus reveal to him in those three lonely days? We may never know exactly, but whatever it was must have been enough truth to relieve Paul of the guilt and shame of his past. My guess? *Jesus revealed to Paul His grace and mercy and Paul's secure place in eternity in heaven.* Once Paul felt Jesus's loving gaze on him, he couldn't look away.

Over and over again—and this is incredible to me—instead of wallowing in guilt for his past mistakes, instead of apologizing again for that which he has already been forgiven, Paul makes his past mistakes a part of his testimony. He doesn't try to hide or bury the fact that he used to be a Pharisee, the fact that he once killed Christians with his own hands; in fact, he repeatedly refers to these things, often calling himself "the worst of sinners"[10] to encourage his followers that if God can use someone as broken as he is, then God can use *anyone.* This is true freedom in Christ!

⌣

WE BAPTIZED OUR son in the Nile River. It's the same river I had chosen to be baptized in at age nineteen. Although I had been a believer and walking with Christ for years before that day, I had never made the decision to be baptized. As I sorted through choosing to surrender my *whole* life—my plans and dreams and future—to God, it felt appropriate that I would also make this public declaration that my whole heart was surrendered and made new in Christ. Many of my children have chosen to be baptized in this very same spot.

In the very river that I thought might take me under during our family camping trip a few months prior, I watched my five-year-old surrender his life to Jesus in the best way he knew how, with his childlike wonder and sweetly trusting belief that He would never let him go.

I stood next to him as his daddy lowered his little body into the water and raised him up again. The look on his face was triumphant as he emerged, his sisters and close friends cheering from the shore. I thought of what we leave behind in the water when we choose to be made new in Christ: our sin, our regret, our failings, our guilt, our shame. I had the startling realization that I had spent the past several years trying to "put back on" things that I had taken off, that Christ had taken for me, all those years ago when my own body was tipped back into the water.

And the more I reclothed myself in these things, the harder it was for me to believe that God delighted in me, that I was His beloved.

Recently, as I lamented my parenting failures to my therapist, she looked straight into my eyes and said, "Katie, you are focusing on the exception, not the rule. Sure, you made mistakes. But you weren't making them all day, every day. In fact, I bet there were so many moments when you were doing things really well." This opened my eyes again to see that the story I was repeatedly telling myself about myself was only a small part of the truth.

Maybe, like I am, you are prone to tell negative stories about yourself or those you love most? Maybe it's in relation to your job or your ministry? Maybe it's in relationship with your spouse? What story are you telling yourself?

If the story you are telling is one in which you are not valuable, one in which you have failed catastrophically or irreversibly screwed everything up, one in which you can trust no one but yourself or you must maintain control at all costs, one in which no one loves you and you are never safe, I want to put my hands on your shoulders, look you in the eyes, and whisper tenderly, "That story is not true."

*There is no failure or mistake that Jesus cannot, will not redeem.* Jesus wants to interrupt these untrue stories just as He interrupted Paul's entire life. He wants to tell us a true story, one in which we are deeply loved, fully forgiven, and completely victorious over the trials of this life.

So, what if we believed Him? What if we started to see ourselves for who we really are: beloved, forgiven, made new? Then we, like Paul, could show up and vulnerably say, "This is me. With all my shortcomings and weaknesses. With all my limitations and failures. The worst of sinners. *And I am beloved of God,* not because of what I've done or what I have failed to do but because He made me and decided to love me."

# 8

---

# PRACTICE MAKES PROGRESS

You will keep in perfect peace
those whose minds are steadfast,
because they trust in you.

—ISAIAH 26:3

"Buddy, let me see your eyes," I say softly for what feels like the hundredth time. It's a phrase often repeated in our house, one I've used with all my children since they were little to make sure that I have their attention.

"I know you really want to play with those puzzle pieces, but I need you to trust Mommy. I need you to trust that I have a good plan." Big sisters are off at summer camp, and I have all kinds of fun planned out for my little guy. But we have to get the last little bit of his kindergarten schoolwork done before we play, and he just won't stop fiddling with the pieces of his puzzle long enough to do the math problems that I know will take him only a few minutes.

I'm frustrated because I know that I have all his favorites in mind; I've been dreaming of all the fun we will have together when it's just me and the littlest two at home for this week. I can't wait to surprise him with so many things that he will love.

"Trust Mommy, bud. I have a really good and fun plan for you if you can just trust and obey. If you can put down the puzzle." As I hear the words coming out of my mouth, I chuckle internally and shake my head a little—he's just like me, just like all of us, really. The puzzle looks fun. He's certain that he has what he wants and that what he has is good (but I know the puzzle doesn't even have all the pieces!). He has no idea of the good plans I have in store for him if he would just drop the puzzle and do some simple addition.

He doesn't want to surrender because he doesn't know what he is missing out on. Maybe the puzzle is as good as it gets. Better hold on tight.

I see myself in my little guy. As I've noted in the past few chapters, so often in my own life I don't want to surrender my control. I don't want to let go of my fears, my coping mechanisms, my plans, or my loved ones because I am not sure what will happen when I do. I have to remind myself over and over again that I am not surrendering to nothing. I am not letting these things go just for the sake of dropping them and not being burdened by them any longer. When I surrender, when I let go, I am placing all that I surrender into the safe and strong hands of my loving God.

AFTER BEING IN the States for several months, we returned to Uganda for a two-week goodbye-for-now visit. I began to sob almost the moment I sat down on my bed there, my mind flooded with memories of pajama-clad toddlers getting ready for bed, rainy-day math lessons while snuggled under blankets, preparations for the births of our babies, and a million late-night chats with my beloved husband. It hit me all over again: I didn't want to surrender *this*. This was all *so good*.

Benji sat and held me for a long time as I cried big ugly tears and wiped my nose on my sweater. (It wasn't cute.) Eventually, my sobs quieted and I walked into the bathroom. The cool tile floor felt familiar under my feet, tile that I have lain on and cried on in desperation, the very floor where I brought my first son into the world, where I have bandaged ouchies and brushed toddler teeth and painted toenails.

There on the mirror was a faded, wrinkled-from-water-droplets lime-green sticky note that read "Lord, You are trustworthy."

The very truth that leads me to trust Him.

The very trust that leads me to surrender.

The very surrender that leads me to peace.

I had scrawled those words in Sharpie during that excruciatingly painful season when our loved one received a life-altering diagnosis and it felt as though our world was collapsing around us. For the next several months, "Lord, You are trustworthy" became a prayer that I needed like oxygen. When my heart was not really believing it, I needed to read it, to say it aloud to myself in the morning, to let it roll around in my brain while I brushed my teeth at night. I would say it, to myself and to Him, throughout the day, knowing that it was true and willing myself to believe it. I wrestled hard to see the faithfulness of the Lord in the chaos.

Even as I had written those words—*Lord, You are trustworthy*—on that sticky note, I had struggled to believe them. Benji had been out of town for months helping our loved one who was fighting for her life. I thought that the trauma of each of my family members' pasts (mine now included) might actually tear us apart. I really and truly wondered if we would make it out of that season with our family and our faith still intact.

Now here we were years later. It hadn't been easy, nothing had gone as I'd expected, but we were okay. God had been faithful. He *had* been trustworthy.

As I acknowledged my reluctance to relinquish my grip on the life and community I'd so loved in Uganda and my reluctance to surrender control at all, I knew it was time to start whispering that prayer again: *Lord, You are trustworthy.*

Trust precedes peace. Trust in God is the basis for everything we need to live lives of peace and steadfastness. As host Tara Leigh Cobble noted in an episode of the *Bible Recap* podcast, "Fear always magnifies the enemy and diminishes God." When I am not trusting, I am walking in fear, and the fear leads me to believe that I am alone, solely responsible for the protection and well-being of my people.

Fear had me gripping my puzzle pieces tight, unwilling to unclench my fists and open my hands and heart to the good plan my loving Father had for me. I realized as I sat there that the desire for control I had worked so hard to surrender had once more taken hold of me during our few months in the United States.

And understandably so. Life was much faster paced than anything I had experienced in fifteen years. Where in Uganda being slightly late was usually acceptable and even sometimes expected, I found that now I was expected to be on time at all costs. Instead of walking leisurely to the local market to pick up whatever ingredients might be available that day, conversing with friends I encountered all along the way, I drove to the store (in a hurry because I was probably late to something), where I was surrounded by hundreds of choices and people I didn't know who were all in a hurry too.

In my determination to keep up and appear to be on top of things despite living in a totally new and unexpected place, I did what I knew how to do. I made lists. I color-coded the calendar and tried to learn to meal plan and bulk grocery shop. Instead of processing the deep grief of leaving behind our familiar life, instead of really digging into the loss of the past season, I managed. I organized. I gave the rest of my family marching orders. It was as if my subconscious were screaming, *We will survive! I will make sure of it!*

Somewhere along the way, I'd determined that I would be the one to solve our problems. I would be the one to keep our kids safe. I would find a way to provide for my family even with our mounting medical bills. I don't like this reality and I am hesitant to type it, but in looking back, I wonder if I grasped at controlling those things because, somewhere deep down, I secretly felt that God hadn't kept up His part. *He hadn't kept us safe.*

Have you found yourself in the same place? We don't want to admit it, but aren't we all a little like the prophet Gideon who looks straight at the face of an angel of the Lord and says, "Pardon me, my lord . . . but if the Lord is with us, why has all this happened to us?"[1]

Thankfully, there is good news again for me—for you—because even though fickle Gideon doubts and waffles and demands signs and questions God, God just keeps assuring Gideon that He will use him anyway, answering again and again, "I will be with you."[2]

⟡

HE WILL BE with us. How do we remind ourselves of this truth when the currents of life send us spinning back into anxiety and fear?

You've probably noticed by now that Jesus had a thing for showing up in the waves. Matthew 8, Mark 4, and Luke 8 all record the story commonly titled "Jesus Calms the Storm." Jesus and His disciples are crossing over from one town to another in a boat when a windstorm sends monstrous waves crashing into it. As the vessel fills with water, Jesus is sound asleep.

I imagine myself stuck in the rapids, the sheer panic, and know this is exactly what I would have felt if I had been in the boat with the disciples. The disciples cry out, much like I did, "Save us, Lord; we are perishing."[3] They've already imagined the worst conclusion. They just know it: *They are going to die.*

Jesus wakes up and looks at them. I imagine His eyes are calm, twinkling. He already knows the disciples are going to be just fine. The first words out of His mouth are "Why are you so afraid?"[4]

Can you imagine Him asking you this question right now? In this season of life, on this busy day, what would you say if Jesus looked right at you and asked tenderly, "Why are you so afraid, my love?"

Many reasons come to my mind:

- I am afraid of failure.
- I am afraid of loss.
- I am afraid of suffering, for myself or those I love.
- I am afraid that God won't heal my loved one who is sick.
- I am afraid I won't parent my children well enough.
- I am afraid I won't love my family well enough.
- I am afraid I am not doing enough.
- I am afraid of the life I have created, which I love, falling apart.
- I am afraid that my days, my life, will not be significant.
- I am afraid that maybe somehow I will mess up God's plan for me or my family.

If this list doesn't resonate with you, fill in your own fears.

Just as I was afraid that my daughter and I would drown in the waves of the river, just as the disciples are afraid that the boat will sink and they will drown in the sea, we are often just afraid that the current of life will take us under. That we won't be enough, that we won't have enough, that we aren't doing enough.

All our vices that rob us of peace—control, distraction, addiction, anxiety—come from a place of fear. And God knows this. God who created us and knows our frame[5] knows that we are scared. He knows it when He makes "Do not be afraid" one of the most frequent commands in all His Word. He knows it when He goes looking for Adam and Eve. He knows that running to hide will be our default, so He asks, "Where are you?" and "Why are you so afraid?"

Mark records that Jesus rose from His sleep and looked at the waves and said, "Peace! Be still!" And just like that, "*there was a great calm.*"⁶ Jesus calms the raging sea and stills the mighty squall with that one word: *peace.*

And isn't this what we are longing for? Isn't this what my heart truly needs? For someone to look at our lists of fears and say to our hearts, "Peace! Be still!" So often, we feel as if we, too, are sinking in the storm as the waves of our everyday lives and responsibilities, struggles, and fears crash all around us. We need a great calm, and we can't muster it up on our own. This peace is available to me and to you because the same God who calmed the wind and the sea, who has power over all nature, has power over our hearts.

Yet how easily we forget that we can safely lean the full weight of our lives on Him. Or at least *I* do.

I believe in Jesus. I walk with Him, I seek Him, and if you asked me if I trust Him, the answer would be a resounding yes. Like I said, I have seen Him provide for my family, part the seas for us again and again. Even so, I, too, often slip back into a way of living that doesn't align with what I know to be true. I find myself swimming hard and fast against the current, having forgotten that He is with me in it.

It seems the more the world around me is spinning, the more the people around me are hurting, the easier it is for me to return to old patterns, where my desperation to control fuels my anxiety, which in turn perpetuates my desire for control. While in some seasons I make great progress in surrendering and trusting, in times of stress I tend to take back the control that I promised to give to God.

I can't be the only one who does this. (Please tell me I am not!)

What if there were a different cycle, though? What if instead of letting our anxiety fuel our control tendencies, which fuel more fear and anxiety, we could lean into a shalom cycle? One that would not leave us feeling pulled apart but instead grounded, whole, complete, steadfast. One in which the more we know God and His trustworthy character, the more we trust Him. The more we trust Him, the more quickly and wholly we surrender, and the more we surrender, the more opportunity we have to see that He never drops anything we give Him, which only increases our trust.

Remember what Isaiah said of God? "You will keep in perfect peace those whose minds are steadfast, because they trust in you."[7] Trust leads to peace.

The more we experience that there is a good, kind, and wise Father looking at us, loving us, delighting in us, making good and careful plans for us, the more we can trust Him. The more we trust Him, the more we'll be willing to surrender. And as we surrender control to this kind and loving God, He will prove time and again that He is worthy of our trust, ultimately leading us to surrender more and more to Him.

He *will* keep us in perfect peace, and this peace comes from learning to trust Him more and more, learning to lay our burdens at His feet and believe that we can leave them there because all our worries and our very lives are safe in His hands. That is the circular way of shalom, a stark contrast to the spiral of anxiety and control that we so often get stuck in.

Just as we see in His encounter with Gideon—who asked that audacious question, the "why?" we feel we often aren't even allowed to utter—the Lord rarely gives a direct answer to why He has allowed the hardship. He simply says again, *I will be with you.*

And in response, Gideon *worships.* He brings the finest of his meat and flour to offer to the Lord. *Our trust is our offering.* And as Gideon recognizes the Lord right there with him in the midst of his questions, God says, "Peace! Do not be afraid," and Gideon builds an altar and names it "The Lord Is Peace."[8]

The Lord is peace.

*Lord, You are trustworthy.*

I THINK ONE of the primary reasons we find ourselves trapped in the anxiety-control cycle is that surrender leaves empty the enormous space our spiraling thoughts once occupied. If we don't fill that space with something, we are going to pick up our same old patterns yet again.

If we revisit that list we made earlier of things that we are struggling to surrender, we might see that we can and do successfully lay them at the feet of Jesus for a season, only to pick them back up a few weeks, days, even minutes later. We are creatures of habit, and control is our addiction. Just like I tell myself that I will stay off my phone during playtime with the kids, only to notice that I keep looking for it or picking it up, I have a habit of surrendering something to Jesus, only to lie awake in bed later that night worrying about that very person or scenario.

As we surrender our worries, our fears, our anxieties, our internal conversations, our tireless planning for unforeseen circumstances, we have to fill the space with something else, and Paul knows just what to do.

"Do not be anxious about anything," he writes to his beloved friends in Philippi. But he doesn't stop there. He gives them instructions on what to do instead, what to replace their anxiety with: "By prayer and petition, with thanksgiving, present your requests to God."[9]

If we are going to trust God, we are going to have to know Him. Once we know Him, we can bring all our hurts, all our worries, all our requests, and all our thanks and praise to His feet. Once we know Him, we can worship. "And the peace of God," Paul promises, "which transcends all understanding, will guard your hearts and your minds in Christ Jesus."[10]

If Jesus Himself is our peace, if indeed peace is a heart shift more than it is an external shift, then we are going to have to learn to trust and surrender and trust some more.

But we are also going to need to practice if we're going to break out of our anxiety-control cycle. We can train our minds; we can set up rhythms in our lives that help us practice this peace.

Although I am still learning what it means to trust even as I write this, in these next chapters, I want to offer some tangible ways we can *practice* trusting God. We need more than a sticky note and a whispered prayer, though it's a good place to start. We need to actively practice the trust that leads us to perfect peace. And while practice doesn't actually make perfect, it does make progress; it does form habits.

What God has in mind for us is so much better than anything we are clinging to, much better than anything we can imagine. Like my little guy clinging to his puzzle pieces with no idea of the good things in store for him, we can loosen our grip. We can surrender in trust to a kind Father who longs for us to experience His joy and peace.

I believe that as we get to know God's character and commune with Him in prayer, as we learn to worship through remembrance, lament, and praise, as we practice presence and stillness and rest and service, God will lead us into the unshakable peace He has promised us.

Eyes on Him, love. The road ahead is long, but we aren't walking it alone.

LET'S PRAY AS we begin this journey together:

*Lord, we confess that we are anxious about many things, and we don't want to be. We confess that we so often want to take control of our lives and our circumstances, even though You have a better plan. We believe that You promise us peace and that You give it to us. We believe that You love us enough to orchestrate Your very best on our behalf, even when we cannot see it. Help us receive this promise and live out of it day by day, moment by moment. We trust You. Amen.*

# 9

## KNOWING HIM

*Practice 1: Spending Time in His Word*

Remain in me, as I also remain in you.

—JOHN 15:4

A t my husband's encouragement, a couple of years ago our family started a one-year Bible-reading plan developed originally by nineteenth-century minister Robert Murray M'Cheyne. It involves no commentaries, no bells and whistles, just the Word. We started with Genesis, Ezra, Matthew, and Acts, reading a chapter of each every day. Some of the reading we did together around the table, and some we did in our own quiet time.

It took me only about a week to realize that *this* was what my heart had been craving: to be immersed in God's Word, reading much larger sections than I had read in a long time. And the more I read, the more I wanted.

I'd recently been in a spiritually dry season, often thumbing through my Bible while asking God to please make it new and exciting to me again. I had picked multiple devotionals up off our bookshelves, only to tire of them after a few short days. *I need You to speak to me,* I'd been whispering to God.

And now I found I was suddenly hungry for these large chunks of time in His Word. *Because He hears the prayers of our weary hearts. Because He longs to be near His people, to remind us of His love for us.*

As I read, I couldn't get over the very obvious truth that the character and magnificence and love of God remained the same through Genesis, Ezra, Matthew, and Acts, and then later through Exodus, Nehemiah, Mark, and Romans, and so on.

Although the daily passages weren't intentionally selected to go together, so often a theme or aspect of God's character came to light in each passage as if it had been handpicked in some kind of topical index. There it was, the Word of God, and my loving Father, the same yesterday, today, and forever. God's character seemed to jump off the page as if to say, *See! He loves you! He has always loved you! He will always love you!* or *Look! He is merciful; He has always been merciful; He will always be merciful.* A generous serving of the peace I had been searching for, grasping for, settled over my heart just in being reminded that God's character doesn't change.

I'd been looking for spiritual encouragement from reading about other people's encounters with God and other people's opinions or interpretations of His Word. And the whole time my old, worn, falling-apart Bible full of stories I thought I already knew was waiting for me to get back to the basics, waiting to reveal new facets of God's character, calling me to set aside my ever-fluctuating emotions and circumstances and rest in the deep peace of my unchanging God.

Morning after morning, I pored over the Word, filling pages of my garage-sale-find college-ruled spiral notebook with evidence of God's mercy and grace and gentleness and love that were the same to Abraham and to the Israelites rebuilding the wall and to the Samaritan woman at the well and to Saul the Pharisee, who became an apostle. And as if it were all new to me, I stood in awe.

As His Word washed over my heart and mind, I began to fix my eyes on the unchanging Giver of Peace rather than on my upended plans and dreams.

⌒

IF WE ARE *going to trust God, first we will have to know Him.* And to know Him, we have to know His Word, where He reveals His character on every page.

Before Jesus began His public ministry of casting out demons and healing and calling people to repentance of sin and to hope for the kingdom that is to come, He spent forty days in the wilderness being tempted by Satan, the very enemy who first whispered the lie to Adam and Eve in the garden. The Gospel of Matthew says that it was the very Spirit of God who led Jesus there,[1] so it wasn't an accident that He faced this temptation. After fasting for forty days and nights, He was understandably hungry. The tempter came to Him and promised what the flesh craved: food, power, *control.* And all three times the devil spoke, Jesus began His counter with three words: "It is written."[2] Jesus, who John calls "the Word" Himself, beat back the Enemy with the very Word of God. Jesus quoted from Deuteronomy, "Man shall not live on bread alone, but on every word that comes from the mouth of God."[3]

We need God's Word like we need bread, sustenance.

Throughout His life, Jesus quoted God's Word in moments of teaching and in times of trial. And if Jesus, perfect, sinless, the very Word Himself, used this Word to combat the Enemy, how much more should we?

In John 15, in the same discourse where Jesus promised His disciples He would leave them with peace, He gave them an instruction to abide in Him. "Remain in me, as I also remain in you," He said. "I am the vine; you are the branches. If you remain in me and I in you,

you will bear much fruit; *apart from me you can do nothing.*"[4] And I know that it is true. When I am disconnected from Jesus, left to spend time with my own fluctuating emotions instead of the truth of His Word, my thoughts spiral quickly into anxiety. If I want to practice walking in peace, I have to prioritize relationship with Him above everything else.

Jesus remains in us by giving us His promised Holy Spirit. We remain *in Him* by spending time in His Word, meditating on His Word, internalizing His Word. God gives us His Word because He longs for us to know His heart.

Often I feel like He is using the passage assigned on a given day of my Bible-reading plan—no matter what plan I happen to be using—to speak directly to my current circumstance, to the very thoughts and emotions of that day. This seems utterly impossible since the plan wasn't written specifically for me and my current situation. But where the reading plan doesn't have me and my personal life and circumstances in mind, God (who does the impossible) *does.* In the New Living Translation, Psalm 139:17 says, "How precious are your thoughts about me, O God. They cannot be numbered!"

What does it do in your heart when you meditate on the truth that not only are God's thoughts better and higher than yours[5] but He thinks *about you*? He wants to reveal specific aspects of His character to you to carry you through these days, this life. He knows your needs even more intimately than you do. And one of the ways He has purposed to provide for our needs is through Scripture.

The Bible says that God's Word is "alive and active."[6] Our personal God, who knows and sees us, who even "chose us in him before the foundation of the world,"[7] uses His Word to minister to our specific needs and life situations.

God has you in mind as He breathes life into His inspired Word. He has us in mind on the mundane, ordinary days with our racing thoughts and emotions that rise and spiral like a river current, threatening to take us under. His thoughts are toward us, and His desire is to use the Word He has already given us to pull us out of the rapids.

J. I. Packer has said about Scripture, "Nobody would know the truth about God, or be able to relate to him in a personal way, had not God first acted to make himself known."[8] God engraved the commandments on stone tablets.[9] He inspired the writers of the Bible to give us His Word.[10] *God wants to be known by us.*

And the more I know of Him, the more I am aware of how much more there is to learn. Because God is infinitely good and kind and wise and powerful, there is no limit to how deeply and intimately I can know Him. Without His Word, we cannot learn to praise Him or live for Him or embrace the peace that is found only in Him.

I KNOW WHAT you might be thinking, because I have thought it a million times before: *I wish I had time to read my Bible more.* During Uganda's first lockdown, I started reading larger chunks of Scripture and journaling as I went. I will admit it was a little easier during that season because *we weren't allowed to go anywhere.* In more "normal" seasons of life, it is so easy to wake up and hit the ground running, doing the necessary and falling into bed at night without cracking open the Bible waiting on the coffee table.

But here is the thing: We need to approach God's Word the same way we approach meals, water, oxygen. *We need it to live.* We need it to walk in the peace that we long for. We can't be vessels that carry His peace and love and goodness to the world unless we know Him, and we can't know Him without spending time learning His character.

I think one of the biggest pitfalls for many of us is this idea that "quiet time," Bible reading, and prayer have to look a certain way. I dream of quiet mornings, alone in the dark before the kids wake up,

## REFRESH YOURSELF IN THE WORD

Psalm 19 says this about the Word of God:

> The law of the LORD is perfect,
>> refreshing the soul.
> The statutes of the LORD are trustworthy,
>> making wise the simple.
> The precepts of the LORD are right,
>> giving joy to the heart.
> The commands of the LORD are radiant,
>> giving light to the eyes.
> The fear of the LORD is pure,
>> enduring forever.
> The decrees of the LORD are firm,
>> and all of them are righteous.
>
> They are more precious than gold,
>> than much pure gold;
> they are sweeter than honey,
>> than honey from the honeycomb.[16]

More precious than gold, sweeter than honey, trustworthy, refreshing, joy giving. This is His Word! But in our noisy, soul-draining world, it doesn't always seem that way.

Have you experienced seasons of life in which God's words feel alive to you and you *want* to pore over them? Have you experienced seasons of dryness, where the Word seems stale and you feel far from God?

Where are you today? What does time in the Word look like for you right now? (There is no shame in admitting that it is nonexistent or inconsistent. I, too, have been in those seasons before, and today can be the day that you remedy that.)

Do you have a set-aside time in the day for being with God? Even if it's sometimes (or often) interrupted, having a designated time will help you remain consistent.

What pockets of quiet in your day are you filling with things such as screen time and scrolling rather than with reading or listening to His Word?

What do you need to do today to get time with God, time in His Word? Maybe you can set aside time before the rest of your household wakes up or during nap time or after the other members of your family go to sleep. Maybe before or after work, before you jump into your daily scrolling, you can open up your Bible. Make this time, no matter what it takes, because lack of it isn't our biggest problem; the Enemy of our souls is.

Decide right now to set aside time to be in God's Word, even if you start small.

- Place your Bible and a journal and pen in a place where you hope to spend time in the Word.
- Download a Bible app and maybe some Bible-focused podcasts for the car. God says that His Word does not return void, so filling our blank spaces and middle minutes with His voice through Scripture will always reap a benefit, even on the days that doesn't feel true.
- Write down a scripture or two that you want to memorize, and place it strategically where you will see it often—maybe above the stove or kitchen sink, on the bathroom mirror, or just above your computer screen.

Man does not live on bread alone. Make sure you are feeding your soul with His Word!

holding a warm cup of coffee and reading my Bible. These moments happen every so often, and they are just as sweet as they sound. But more often than not, this isn't how it goes.

Over the course of the past fifteen years, I have encountered every season of parenting. We have had teenagers who stay up late to write papers and get out the door early for school, and I've been up with them, late and early. We have had babies who just did not sleep, leaving me trying to sneak in some rest for myself in those early-morning hours. There have been seasons when I have consistently been able to find my spot on the couch in the morning with my Bible, and plenty more when I haven't.

I distinctly remember one day a few years ago when I had woken up early to beat the morning rush, feeling desperate for the Lord and excited for time with Him. As I cracked open my Bible and my jour-nal, little feet pattered down the hallway and our youngest curled up on my lap, right on top of the Bible I had just opened. While some mornings he is content to quietly read or play beside me, this morn-ing he needed a snack. Then a new diaper. Then help fixing his Lego house. He wanted me to read him a book and I said, "Just one." Then he was hungry again. The rest of the family woke up and some raced out the door for school. I took my Bible with me to the kitchen while I set the table for breakfast with the homeschoolers. A friend popped in to drop off her toddler for us to babysit.

I won't burden you with details of the rest of the day, but you can imagine where this is going. One thing led to another, and I kept dragging my opened Bible around the house with me, trying to read a line here and there between each activity. Eventually, a few of my girls got to a place in their school assignments where they could work independently, and I spread a blanket on the floor for the littles with books and crayons and reread the passage that I had been read-ing verse by verse all morning. It was Galatians 6, and right there in the middle, it jumped off the page: "Let us not become weary in doing good, for at the proper time we will reap a harvest if we do not give up."[11]

I could have been frustrated that I wasn't getting the me time I needed with my Bible, but here was a reminder to simply be grateful for this living and active Word in front of me. Here was evidence that, just as Jesus multiplied bread and fish to feed five thousand, He could multiply this Word in my heart as I moved throughout my day.

God has so much grace for the busy days. I believe that even if I hadn't gotten to finally read Galatians 6 on the day that I just described, God would have been honored by my trying and my desire to show up and be present with Him even though really necessary stuff kept getting in the way. But my day was better because I made time to do it. Somewhere in my life or the lives of my children, there will be a harvest because I keep doing my best to prioritize His Word even when it would be easier to give up.

Do not grow weary, dear one. We can't give up on seeking the Lord and carving out time with Him in our daily lives, even when it doesn't work out as we plan.

Psalm 103:14 says, "[God] knows our frame; he remembers that we are dust" (ESV). He knows what the days require of us, what we are capable of and what we aren't.

And here is the beauty of it: God is honored by a heart that seeks Him, and He can meet you exactly where you are. You don't have to be curled up on the couch with your coffee, even though that's my favorite way to do it. I've read verses on the Bible app on my phone while nursing babies in my rocking chair or while waiting in the car for big kids to get out of school. I've listened to the audio Bible while getting ready for work, while driving to work, while chopping carrots and potatoes for stew. I also love listening to various podcasts and teaching from Christian leaders. I've dragged my worn Bible with me all over the house and out to the swing set and into the garden and with me to the grocery store and the doctor's office just in case I might have the opportunity to crack it open. I leave it on the coffee table, on my desk, on the kitchen counter with a journal and pencil beside it for moments with Him in between the busyness of the day.

Nothing beats uninterrupted time in His Word whenever you can get it, but if you are in a season when that doesn't seem possible, don't let that deter you. You can make time to know Him. And as you know Him, as you abide in His Word, His peace will abide in your heart.

I AM ONE of those people who rocks their babies to sleep. Yep. Every. Single. Time. My first baby girl basically lived in the baby carrier, strapped to my chest for the first three years of her life. She would easily nap there, and even long after she had transitioned to napping in a crib, if I needed her to fall asleep quickly or in a new or unusual place, I could strap her to me and she would be gently snoring in no time.

When she was really little, at nap time I would put her in the carrier and walk around our little neighborhood, reciting whatever Scripture I was memorizing with my bigger kids at homeschool. Often these scriptures were accompanied by a tune meant to help with memorization, and I would hum the song as we walked.

You can imagine how surprised I was when at two years old, my baby girl, no more than twenty pounds, started spouting off long sections of Scripture. She had internalized and memorized all of Romans 5 as we walked around the neighborhood together for her nap and I whispered or sang it above her head.

By the time my next baby was born, though, I had a smartphone. My son preferred to be rocked to sleep in a chair, and I noticed that I often filled that time scrolling through my phone, comparing my life to everyone else's or catching up on work or email. This particular baby didn't sleep well or often, so we spent many hours in that rocking chair.

A friend challenged me to use that time to memorize Scripture instead of catching up on work or scrolling aimlessly. I wrote down the scriptures I wanted to memorize and hung them on the walls of the little closet-turned-nursery where we rocked. I set verses as the screen saver on my phone so that if I was tempted to scroll, I would be again reminded of the truth I so desperately longed to internalize.

I had no idea that, years later, all my nap-time and bedtime scriptures would come flooding back to help me battle my anxious thoughts. As my heart and mind began to spin, I would whisper the words to Psalm 91, a portion of which says this:

I will say of the LORD, "He is my refuge and my fortress,
    my God, in whom I trust."

Surely he will save you
    from the fowler's snare
    and from the deadly pestilence.
He will cover you with his feathers,
    and under his wings you will find refuge;
    his faithfulness will be your shield and rampart.[12]

Salvation. Shalom. Peace.

When we study and memorize Scripture, we are memorizing pieces of God's character the way I have memorized the wrinkles around my daddy's eyes when he laughs or the curve of my infant's milk-white fingernails as his tiny fingers curl around mine. We come to know Him. And when we know Him, His words and assurance and peace rise up in our hearts and minds even as the world around us spins, even as we are pummeled by the waves. He Himself is our peace, remember?[13] His Word centers us, brings us back to wholeness, to shalom.

"Remain in me," Jesus says, "as I also remain in you."[14] Is it possible that Jesus isn't just in the boat with us but that in many ways He *is* the boat, carrying us safely through the storm?

In Acts 4, Peter and John are imprisoned for sharing the Gospel. The local authorities seem to think that a few good beatings and a couple of imprisonments will be enough to deter them, but instead the apostles persevere against persecution and continue preaching the good news. Luke records that the rulers and authorities were astonished by the courage of Peter and John. In fact, Scripture says that when the rulers witnessed the boldness of Peter and John, they thought, *These men must have been with Jesus.*[15]

In my own life I want to live in such a way, with such courage and grace and sincerity that all who encounter me think, *She must have been with Jesus.* And in order for that to be true, I need to fill my mind and my heart and my days with Him. I want people to look at my life and see Jesus in me. I want to live in a way that points others toward Him.

And it all starts in His Word.

We start with His Word. We read it. We internalize it. We dwell on it, abiding in Him and He in us. And the more we know of it, the more we can speak it. We can speak it to our own spiraling thoughts, we can speak it as encouragement to a friend or neighbor, and we can speak it back to our loving Father, not to remind Him of who He is but to remind ourselves.

*Father, thank You for the gift of Your Word. Thank You for longing to reveal Yourself to Your people and for giving us*

*this tool so that we can know You. We are amazed by Your character, Your goodness, and Your depth, Lord. We ask that You would draw us to Yourself, that You would make Your Word come alive for us. Turn our eyes and our hearts toward You and allow us to live in the peace that comes from knowing and resting in Your character. We love You, Father. Amen.*

# 10

## OUR CLOSEST FRIEND

*Practice 2: Spending Time in Prayer*

Draw near to God, and he will draw near to you.

—JAMES 4:8, ESV

"I need to walk." It's a kind of SOS text message that I've been sending to my best friend for nearly two decades. When she lived down the street from me, she inevitably would show up within the next thirty minutes, sneakers laced and stroller ready. These days she lives an ocean away, but sometimes I still send the text, put on my shoes, and pull out FaceTime. "I need to walk," I text, but what I really mean is "I need to talk." I need to share my heart with someone who knows me—all of me—and loves me anyway.

I got to spend a week with this dear friend a few months ago. We walked and talked, laughed and cried. I don't think I realized just how unlike myself I'd been feeling until we were together and everything felt right again.

It is amazing how, in the midst of the dark and the hard, someone who truly knows us can remind us of who we really are, remind us of what is true, when we are drowning in a current of spiraling thoughts and wonderings and emotions. We need this. I am deeply grateful to have a few amazing people in my life who do this for me.

I cried a lot harder than I expected to when I hugged my bestie goodbye and kissed her daughter's soft cheeks. But as I sat in the silence after they headed home, a thought occurred to me that gave me the greatest comfort: Our God wants to do this for each of us, to remind us not only of who we truly are in Him but also of who He is and to remind us of what is true—His ultimate truth—when the rapids of our thoughts and emotions threaten to overtake us. The God who knows us more intimately than even our closest friend, who knows our frame and our frailty, wants to meet with us, wants to remind us of His power and love and grace. Just as all feels right in the world when I sit next to my bestie and watch our kids play, when I sit with God, He makes things right again.

It is simple but true, when my mind is racing and my heart is thumping, that I can send out that same SOS to my loving Father: *I need to talk.* As my head hits the pillow at the end of an overfull day or as I wake up in the morning already feeling overwhelmed, I call out to Him, *I need to meet with You.* And even more quickly than the most loyal friend, there He is.

He *wants* to meet with me, and with you. He wants to remind us of who we are. Even more than that, He wants to remind us of who *He* is, the One in whom all our comfort, hope, and peace rest.

And this happens only when we intentionally make time for Him. As we saw in the previous chapter, we study His Word to learn His character and who He is. As we come to know Him, our understanding of His character can inform our prayers, our conversations with Him, our "walks" with Him that can become sweeter than time with even the closest of friends. More precious than gold and sweeter than honey, remember?

You know those friends—like my best friend—who can basically just take the words right out of your mouth? The ones you hardly have to say anything to and they already know what you are thinking and feeling? Psalm 139 says,

O LORD, you have searched me and known me!
You know when I sit down and when I rise up;
    you discern my thoughts from afar.
You search out my path and my lying down
    and are acquainted with all my ways.
Even before a word is on my tongue,
    behold, O LORD, you know it altogether.[1]

God knows our words before they form on our tongues; He knows our thoughts, our feelings, our sins, our hearts. There is no friend closer than this.

THE NUMBER ONE question I get asked on social media isn't about the size of my family or about overseas missions or ministry. What people seem to want to know more than anything else is this: "With such a full life, how do you find time with Jesus?"

Here's my honest answer, without a hint of sarcasm or sass: I find time with Jesus because *I have to*. Because I have tried over and over to do life on my own (you know, my control thing), and I know better than anyone that *I can't*. Because I have messed this up a thousand times, and I can tell you that when I am not spending time with Him, you *don't* want to spend time with me.

Even so, I don't always do it well. I cannot tell you the number of times I have crawled out of bed in the morning excited to grab a cup of coffee and spend some time with my Bible or speaking to God in prayer but have picked up my phone instead. One message leads to another. I quickly check and respond to a few emails. I decide to see what the world is up to on Instagram and fall down a rabbit hole and end up watching or reading something I am not even that interested in. Before I know it, half an hour has gone by and the kids need breakfast or school help, and just like that the day is off to a running start with my mind filled with what's going on in everyone else's seemingly perfect life—or, worse, filled with the latest disaster of our fallen world—instead of with what God has to say about my life and His plans and purposes.

I know it's not the best way to start my day. I know it's not the best way to fill my heart and mind so that I can pour peace into my children and the others God puts in my path throughout the day, but it is such an easy pattern to fall into.

Maybe you can relate. Perhaps you, too, wake with the best intentions of making time with God a priority, but before you know it, your mind and your heart are filled with other things. What is distracting you from time with Him? What *feels* more appealing than talking to God at the start of your day and throughout your day?

My heart ached a little as I typed that out. I am asking myself those questions too. If the Word of God is more precious than gold, then surely time spent in His presence is as well. He is worthy of so much more than all the affection I could send His way, worthy of my attention and adoration every minute of every day that I live.

After years of fighting against the pull of technology and a glittery world to have set-apart time with God, I have decided this: If we want it to happen, we just have to make it happen. We must prioritize our time with the Lord as if our very lives depend on it, *because they do*. We need to be with Jesus every single day. We need to pour out our hearts to Him.

I could tell countless stories, and my husband and children could too, about how quickly the day unravels when I have tried to go it alone without prioritizing Jesus and asking for His help. I can so quickly crush a child's spirit with wrong words or even a glance; I can get angry at my husband for absolutely nothing; I can let my thoughts spiral into melodramatic what-if scenarios.

Jesus wants to keep us from these frantic days and moments, but

He can do that only if we turn our hearts attentively to Him. The Bible promises that if we draw near to God, He will draw near to us.[2] So how do we draw near? Remember Paul's direction to the Philippians about how to replace anxiety with something more productive? "In everything *by prayer and supplication,* with thanksgiving, let

## WORDS WITH A FRIEND

While I love starting my morning in prayer and God's Word, God doesn't need or want to be relegated to a specific portion of our lives. He is in all of it! When we whisper to Him in the ordinary middle minutes of our days, we will find that He meets us where we are.

It sounds simple enough, but stopping to pray throughout my entire day instead of making prayer a once-a-day, specific-amount-of-minutes, structured quiet time helps me redirect my thoughts toward Him and, in doing so, redirect my anxiety and reclaim my day by being present.

I believe that the more time we spend falling in love with our gracious God, understanding the richness, beauty, and kindness of His character, the more quickly our hearts will turn toward Him with our needs, secrets, hurts, and longings. And with our anxiety as well.

How would it change the way we approach God if we truly believed He wanted to meet with us? If we began to call Him, speak to Him like a treasured friend, and knew He cared to listen to every little detail? It might drastically alter our relationship, moving Him from someone we view as far-off and unavailable to a God who calls us by name, who desires both to listen to us your requests be made known to God."[3] We bring our hearts, our requests, our petitions to Him.

I know you are busy. *I* am busy. And I have spent long seasons of my life believing that I was "too busy" to spend chunks of time studying Scripture and praying. And if I could have coffee with myself as a

---

and speak to us. We might say with Jacob, "I saw God face to face."[6]

So, friend, let's try it. Find a quiet place for a moment and try whispering, "I need to talk." The God you are looking for is looking back at you with love in His eyes, ready to listen, ready to speak.

Allow Him to remind you who He created you to be:

- His beloved child[7]
- A dear friend of His[8]
- A new creation[9]
- Crowned with love and compassion[10]
- Abounding in love and mercy[11]

Allow Him to remind you of who *He is:*

- "Surely God is my help; the Lord is the one who sustains me."[12]
- "The LORD is the everlasting God, the Creator of the ends of the earth. He does not faint or grow weary; his understanding is unsearchable."[13]
- "The LORD is gracious and compassionate, slow to anger and rich in love."[14]

We could fill pages with evidence of His good character and His love for us!

young mother, I would reach across the table and grab her hand and say, "I know. I know you are so busy loving and serving and doing *important* things. But all your loving and serving and ministry has to flow out of your time with God or it will amount to nothing."

Jesus models this so beautifully.

In Mark 6, before the story we looked at earlier where Jesus gets in the boat with His disciples, Jesus is hurting. He's probably tired. He's been traveling all over the region, often without a place to lay His head, serving, healing, teaching, and continually pouring Himself out for those He loves. When He hears that His cousin John has been beheaded, all He wants to do is gather His disciples to Himself and go away to a quiet place to rest, to be still and seek His Father. But as they are going, the crowd surrounds them. Jesus is interrupted, just as you and I are so often. And instead of annoyance, which I confess is often my first reaction, Jesus has compassion on those who are interrupting His great and God-honoring plans to get away for some time with the Father.

He stops. He teaches them. He feeds them. Of course, it's a lot cooler than what's probably going on in your day-to-day or mine, because He is Jesus and because He miraculously feeds five thousand people, while I am often just trying to figure out the one food that my toddler will eat on a given day. But boiled down to the very basics, this is pretty similar to what happens to you and me on a daily basis. I want to seek the Lord, I want to have time with Him, but . . . *people*. I get interrupted by people who have real needs that I am called to meet.

What we can learn from Jesus in this passage (among a host of other things) is persistence to make time with God in prayer a priority. Once everyone has eaten their fill and headed home, Jesus sends His disciples on ahead of Him so that He can go up on the mountainside to pray.[4]

*He has to be with His Father.*

In fact, Jesus often went away by Himself to pray. Mark 1:35 says that Jesus got up early in the morning while it was still dark and went away to a solitary place to pray. Luke 6:12 talks about Jesus going up on a mountain and spending the whole night in prayer. The Gospels even record some of the prayers of Jesus when He stopped in the middle of what He was doing to give thanks or petition His Father. Remember, He is Jesus: perfect, sinless, God incarnate. So if He needs time to connect with the Father, how much more do we?

SOON AFTER WE moved our family from Uganda to the United States, I decided, *Each morning, I am not getting out of bed until I pray.* Honestly, for those first few months, I couldn't get out of bed without a lot of prayer, and even then it felt like a struggle. I yearned to move my mind and heart out of my anxiety spiral and into a place of shalom, and I knew it had to start with Him.

Each morning, I would wake up in the unfamiliar light-blue bedroom of our temporary housing, which had undoubtedly been a provision of the Lord but still didn't feel like home. As I opened my eyes, a wave of panic and dread would wash over me. *This isn't my house. This isn't my home. I have to get up and live here another day.* It was enough to make me want to pull the covers back over my head and stay there. But the responsibility of having children eliminated staying in bed for the day as an option. So instead I began to pray.

Before I crawled out of bed, I would call to mind something I knew to be true about God's character (even on the days it didn't *feel* true or felt too good to be true). *You are kind, Lord. We have seen Your kindness, and I believe You will be kind again today.* Or, *You are our provider, God. I see the ways You provided for Your people throughout history and the ways You are providing for us here and now. I trust You to continue to give us what we need.* And then I would end with some version of this, sometimes just a feeble whisper: *This day is Yours, Lord. I need You. Help me. Lead me. I give You control.*

I know it sounds simple, but it has made a profound difference for me. Beginning the day this way stopped my thought spiral before it even began, shifted my eyes from my own self-pity and lack to who God is and His abundant goodness. Slowly but surely, I began to feel content. Even though my current situation wasn't changing, *my heart was.*

And I don't need these prayers just in the morning; I need them throughout the day, hourly, sometimes minute by minute. I've learned that when I feel my head and my heart racing forward to the future, I can pause and cry out to God: *I need You to still my heart. I need You to take care of [whatever future decision/scenario is worrying me]. I believe that You will.* When my thoughts begin to swirl like the rapids on the Nile, threatening to take me under, I imagine the view from the bank and envision my loving Father, who can see the whole path and the whole plan, assuring me that all will be well because it will all be exactly as He intended.

Left to my own devices, I am hardwired to turn inward. It takes a lot of practice to turn instead toward a loving God. But when we do turn toward Him, when we allow our eyes to find His, I imagine Him as the delighted parent who notices her toddler glancing at her from across the room or her teen looking for her from the basketball court. I imagine Him as the loving father scanning his fields for his prodigal son to return. Because that is who He is.

Remember all those places I mentioned before, where I've pulled out my Bible app to read Scripture or whisper it under my breath? I've prayed in all those places too: Kroger checkout lines and kids' basketball games and Target bathroom stalls. *God, I need You. I need to talk to You.* When I find myself aimlessly replaying a hard conversation in my head for the fifth time, thinking of all the things I should have said and the things I wish I hadn't said, when I start to spiral in worry or frustration about a child's behavior or future, when I see the pile of dishes in the sink and feel resentful, wondering if anyone even sees or cares that I just tidied the house *again,* I can turn my eyes and my heart toward Him. He can, and will, replace my thoughts with His thoughts[5]—I need Him to.

RECENTLY, I WAS freaking out about a situation with a certain loved one. I've been there before. I know that it's not what I want to do, and I know that it isn't helpful. But once again, I found myself caught in my spiral, and I lay awake long into the night, worrying.

When sleep finally came, it was fitful and interspersed with dreams of me carrying this loved one (an adult who is much taller than I am, by the way) very awkwardly. I'd carry her to the car and then carry her to the doctor. I'd carry her to various appointments and classes and meetings. In my dream, we stumbled around, sometimes falling, me heaving to scoop up her heavy, lifeless body, sometimes half carrying and half dragging her to where she needed to be. Or where I *thought* she needed to be anyway. As I rushed with her from one place to another, I was very aware that we were late and that maybe it would not be enough and maybe it was all for nothing.

I woke up filled with anxiety over all the carrying I had done, or failed to do. As I let myself slowly come to the realization that this dream, while vivid, was not real life, I also became deeply aware that although I was not *actually* carrying anyone, this was exactly what I often wanted to do. Not just for this loved one but for all my children, family members, and friends, and even many I don't know well who are enduring injustice and hardship.

In my dream, and in my thoughts the day before, I had decided that I would take control. If she didn't see what was best for her life, I would. If God wouldn't do it for her (*for me!*), I would do it myself. Ugh. I've mentioned that I'm a work in progress, right?

As I sat there on the edge of the bed, still trying to untangle such a vivid dream from reality, I felt God whisper to my spirit, *Carry her to Me. Carry them all to Me.*

I'm tearing up a little as I type this because God is so gracious and giving up control is *still* so hard for me sometimes. But I know He is right. Prayer is our first point of surrender. For our plans and our dreams and our heart's desires and also of those we love so dearly that we would give our very lives to protect them. When we *can't* control and we can't fix and we can't help in the way that we hoped, we can carry those we care most about to Jesus—and not only our hurting loved ones. Prayer is how we carry our best-laid plans and our broken dreams and our deep regret and our giant mess to Jesus. And to do so, we have to make time with Him a priority. If we don't, our anxious thoughts stay swirling in our heads. Talking to Him is a crucial part of our shalom cycle: know Him, trust Him, surrender to Him, practice peace.

So this is where you will find me most mornings: still in bed with the covers pulled over my head or nestled in the corner of my couch or sometimes hiding in the walk-in closet, always with eyes closed and palms up, fists unclenched, praying my desperate prayers, giving God the control that my sin nature wants to clasp tight, knowing that it was never mine to begin with. Remembering what is true. Remembering who is really in control. Remembering His character.

God is faithful to answer prayers and will *always* answer when we pray for His will. Of course, it is His will to be in control of our days and our lives, to lead us and help us. We ask Him for these things not to change His mind—He has already purposed to do these things—but to change our hearts toward Him. When we come to Him with a surrendered heart posture, He is glorified and our own desires are slowly changed and formed to His desires for us.

Friend, don't believe the lie that you are too busy to be with the Lord, to talk to Him, to hear from Him. Don't buy into the mentality that you will prioritize Him later or spend more time with Him in another season. And don't buy into the thinking that you need fifteen minutes with God in the morning and, *check,* you're done for the day. We need Him like we need breath. We need Him while we scrub the toilets and while we fold the laundry and while we drive to work and while we chop the veggies for supper. We need Him when things are going really well, and especially when they aren't.

We make time for Jesus with such a full life because our peace depends on it. *Our very lives depend on it.*

God wants to meet with you here and now. In the school pickup line. On the floor surrounded by Lego pieces and stuffed animals. Today, in the middle of the mess and the busyness, in the middle of the noise and all that you are responsible for, He desires to speak to you, to commune with you, to fill you with His peace.

*How precious, Lord, that we can call You "friend"! May we be quick to turn to You and cry out to You when the waves around us crash, when the rapids of life spin chaotically. We are easily distracted, turning to what we think we need instead of what we truly need: time with You. Help us, Father! We long to trust You deeply and live in Your peace, and we need Your help. Speak to our hearts. May we find our refuge and our safety in You, our deep and perfect peace. We love You, Lord. Amen.*

# 11

## STONES AND BREAD

### *Practice 3: Remembering*

Remember that you were slaves in Egypt and that the LORD your God brought you out of there with a mighty hand and an outstretched arm.

—DEUTERONOMY 5:15

Over the past months, God has often brought to mind our frightening experience on the river. I sometimes pull out my photo of that river bend and remember how it felt to be in the water, nearly drowning, imagining the worst. Then I recall what it was like to stand at the top of the bank, the Nile in all its splendor twisting below me, able to see the whole path and know that I was safe.

I hold those images in my mind as I reflect on the past several years—the first medical crisis that sent me spinning, yes, but also the way our friends and neighbors rallied around us. They brought coffee and dinner, words of prayer and encouragement. They came and sat with me, sometimes with wise counsel and other times in comforting silence, just so that I would not be alone.

I think of all the *unbelievable* ways God provided for our family in our life in Uganda, times He quite literally saved our lives. I remember our recent transition to the States and all the ways God had so clearly provided for us: a home, a community, more time together as a family, *joy in this place.*

Yet all too often, in my determination to forge ahead and keep everything going, *I have forgotten.* I am an Israelite, calling for meat when God has given manna,[1] sustenance, exactly what I have needed, what our family has needed, over and over again.

"I will remember the deeds of the LORD," Asaph writes in Psalm 77. "I will remember your miracles of long ago. I will consider all your works and meditate on all your mighty deeds."[2] When Asaph cannot see or feel God in his present circumstance, he remembers who God is and what He has done before.

And I'm learning that this is one of the practices I can put into action when I'm struggling to surrender, to trust, to believe the true story of who God is and how He loves me.

THROUGHOUT ALL OF Scripture, both the Old Testament and the New, God calls His people to remember His past faithfulness.

In Genesis 28, years before Jacob wrestles with God, as he runs from the brother who has sworn to kill him for stealing the blessing he believed was his birthright, God speaks to him in a dream and promises to preserve and prosper him. When Jacob wakes up, he says, "Surely the LORD is in this place, and I was not aware of it. . . . This is none other than the house of God; this is the gate of heaven."[3]

*God is working, even where we least expect He could be.* Our unexpected, unwanted, uncertain circumstances can be a place where we experience God, can be a gate to see His goodness.

Jacob takes the stone that he slept on and sets it up as a pillar, a remembrance of the Lord meeting him there. He names the pillar *Bethel,* which means "house of God." God was here in this unexpected place, Jacob says, and *he is going to remember.*

Years later, God has fulfilled many of His promises to Jacob. Jacob has married and had children, he has met with Esau and received abundant grace and forgiveness, and now God instructs him to re-turn to Bethel, to the stone he set up to remember how He had spo-ken to him.[4]

God seems to say, *Remember where I brought you from so that you can trust Me for where I am taking you next.*

I wonder if Jacob wept when he saw the stone, when he realized that God had indeed cared for him through all the twist and turns, through all the highs and lows, through all the victories and unex-pected hardships. What we do know is that when Jacob reaches Bethel, when Jacob sees that stone, *he worships.*

Remembering God's past faithfulness is an act of trust and an act of worship. As we remember all the ways He has loved us, cared for us, and provided for us in the past, we see once again that we can trust Him with our futures, no matter how uncertain they may seem.

I think often of Moses leading arguably the most obstinate, dis-trusting group of people in human history through the wilderness for forty years. They spent forty years making a journey that should have taken them *eleven days.* If I am honest, I can't imagine how ex-asperated I would have been in Moses's shoes. I would have been yelling the marching orders and racing ahead of these stubborn peo-ple, willing them to keep up, get it right, stop being so foolish. Yet Moses (though imperfect) is filled with compassion for these foolish people, just as God is filled with compassion for those He calls His own.

In the first chapters of Deuteronomy, Moses recounts to the Isra-elites the faithfulness of the Lord. *Remember, remember,* he says. He speaks of God's intentionality, of God's provision for His people and His protection of them through much hardship. Even though they have been traveling for forty years and it would be so easy to wonder if God had completely forgotten them, Moses still speaks confidently of "the good land the LORD your God is giving you."[5] He doesn't lose hope, even in promises that he can't see, because he so deeply and truly *trusts* his Father.

He remembers where they have been so that he can believe God will bring them to where they are going. For basically their entire forty-year journey in the wilderness, Moses reminds the Israelites of what God has done for them and who He has been.

> Do not be terrified; do not be afraid of them. The LORD your God, who is going before you, will fight for you, as he did for you in Egypt, before your very eyes, and in the wilderness. There you saw how the LORD your God carried you, as a father carries his son, all the way you went until you reached this place.[6]

Moses speaks this truth and many similar exhortations over the Israelites to remind them who God is. He remembers, and urges them to remember, all that God has done for them.

- *Remember when He fought for us in Egypt?*
- *Remember how He provided for us in the wilderness?*
- *Remember how He carried us in the desert?*

God had carried them like a father carries his small child. He had protected them and provided for them through the harrowing wilderness with water springing out of rocks and food falling from the sky!

For their entire journey, they had everything they needed. I always find my heart moved when I read Deuteronomy 29, where the Lord Himself says, "Your clothes did not wear out, nor did the sandals on your feet."[7] Forty years is a long time to walk in the same pair of sandals. But God never abandons His people, and He is concerned with even the smallest of details, like the comfort of their feet and the condition of their clothing. He is so personal. So intimate.

And our sinful nature is hardwired to forget. To complain. To live distracted.

I pause and ask myself,

- *Remember how He has fought for you and for your children?*
- *Remember how He provided for us when we didn't have what we needed?*
- *Remember how He parted the seas for us, making a way where there didn't seem to be one?*
- *Remember how He carried us when our legs couldn't walk on their own anymore?*
- *Remember all the abundantly good gifts and sweet days and precious laughter and deep relationships He has given even in the middle of the hard?*

I can testify too: He has carried me, carried me like a father carries his small child, all the way until I reached this place, today. And when I remember, I sit in awe. He is the tenderest Father.

Can you ask yourself these same questions, friend? Even if you can't see how He might provide for you in your current situation or how He might make a way through your current wilderness, can you look back and see that He has never left you? And if that is true, isn't it also true that He never will? What would shift in your perspective on today's difficulties if you chose to remember His past faithfulness and focus on that rather than the difficulty ahead?

In the midst of my own trials and frustrations, I've found that remembering who He is, what He has done for His people, and what He has done for *me* and my people stills my racing heart and causes me to believe that He will do it again. He will provide again. He will

## HISTORICAL MARKERS

Where are you struggling to trust God today? Where are you doubting? Can you remember other similar situations He has carried you through? What are your stones of remembrance, the markers of your journey with a faithful God, reminding you that He is trustworthy?

Call to mind a time when God came through for you. If you are like me, one memory might lead to another. Spend some time remembering all He has done for you, times when He has answered your prayers.

Write these things down. Even better, grab a friend or your child or spouse and speak out loud to one another stories of God's provision in your life and times that He has come through.

As you reflect on your testimony of God's goodness to you, try to identify some tangible stones of remembrance you can look at or hold on to when you need a reminder of His past faithfulness to help you face the future with firm confidence in your Traveling Companion.

Journaling is a wonderful practice in remembering. I confess, I am not as consistent with it as I would like to be, but I always appreciate when I can flip through an old journal and be reminded of God's faithfulness in so many small ways throughout my days, weeks, and years.

Maybe this is the day you begin journaling for just a few minutes daily about the things God is doing in your life, the things you are hoping for, the things you are grieving. One day you will look back and see stories of His goodness and faithfulness all over your life. I am sure of it.

make a way again. It might not be a way out of the hardest places—in fact, it might be a way straight through the wilderness—but He will be with us again. He will not leave. *He never leaves.*

After Moses dies and Joshua is about to lead the Israelites into the Promised Land following their forty years of wandering in the desert, God stops the racing flow of the Jordan River to allow His people to cross into their new home, mirroring His parting of the Red Sea for their parents and grandparents as they fled from the Egyptians. God then instructs Joshua to make a memorial there, to mark the place with twelve stones so that

> when your children ask their fathers in times to come, "What do these stones mean?" then you shall let your children know, "Israel passed over this Jordan on dry ground." For the LORD your God dried up the waters of the Jordan for you until you passed over . . . so that all the peoples of the earth may know that the hand of the LORD is mighty, that you may fear the LORD your God forever.[8]

He did it so that they would remember. *So that they would remember to trust Him.* Years later, when God enabled the Israelites to defeat the Philistines, the prophet Samuel set up a stone near the side of the battle and said, "Thus far the LORD has helped us."[9]

We can begin to panic as we look forward, but if we look back, we are bound to see—thus far the Lord has helped us. When the current spiraled and when the waves crashed. When we should have been wrecked, ruined, utterly destroyed. He held us fast. He carried us like a father carries a child.

God is always bringing us back, always prompting us to remember. As we remember where He has carried us, we can trust that He will continue. God, who never left Jacob, who never left His chosen people, who has never left me, is not going to leave us now. We can trust Him. In fact, we must.

IF WE WERE sitting together right now and I asked you about God's past faithfulness, what story would you tell me? Where, I would love to know, have you witnessed God's goodness to you, to those you care most about? If you're out of practice, it may take a bit to bring examples to mind, but I promise that the encouragement to you, and to those with whom you share your story, is well worth the effort.

I'm convinced there is something truly profound about testifying to the ways the Lord has been good to us. We aren't just remembering for ourselves; we are telling others, remembering publicly, recounting the good and kind ways of our Father to remind them that He is going to be this same good and kind Father to them too.

Individually and collectively remembering, recounting His faithfulness, reminds our hearts that He will continue to provide for us. Psalm 78 urges us to "tell to the coming generation the glorious deeds of the LORD."[10] Through our testimony of His faithfulness, we are reminded, our children are inspired, to "set their hope in God."[11]

When we look back, when we share with one another our experience of God's faithfulness, we can see more and more reasons to trust Him for whatever lies ahead. Jacob, Moses, Joshua, and Samuel *remember* who God is, who He was, and what He has done before so that they—and those they are leading—can trust Him for what is up ahead, for what they cannot yet see.

Even with so much proof of God's love and provision, even with so many instances to remember how He cared for and protected them, the Israelites still often struggle or even completely fail to trust Him. I, too, have often diverted my eyes from Him, looking instead to the storm around me, and this is when I get stuck in fear instead of the peace that comes from deep trust.

And even in all the Israelites' doubt, even in all of mine, God continues to seek after His people, to pursue them, to love and provide for and protect them. We are a forgetful people. *And God knows it.*

On the night he was betrayed, [Jesus] took bread, and when he had given thanks, he broke it and said, "This is my body, which is for you; do this in remembrance of me." In the same way, after supper he took the cup, saying, "This cup is the new covenant in my blood; do this, whenever you drink it, in remembrance of me." For whenever you eat this bread and drink this cup, you proclaim the Lord's death until he comes.[12]

Jesus knows we are just like the Israelites. He knows that even the very disciples who stand next to Him while He dies on the cross, the very men who see Him resurrected and place their hands in the wound on His side, who touch the nail holes in His hands—even they will need a tangible and concrete reminder of what He has done for us.

And He chooses bread and wine, things so commonplace, so ordinary, that His people would see them every day to remember Him. "Take and eat," He says.[13] *Partake of Me so that you might remember Me. Remember Me so that you will continue to trust Me.*[14]

Our physical beings need physical reminders, and God is faithful to provide them. He gives us rainbows in the sky and words we can memorize and bread we can swallow. His people set up stones and build altars.

When I look back over these past years, I see where He has parted seas in my life. He has been good and faithful.

*Lord, You are trustworthy.*

I still keep in my Bible that little green sticky note from the bathroom mirror even though it is too old and worn to stick to anything anymore. I keep it because it helps me remember. I even made a new one and stuck it on the mirror of our rental house in Tennessee.

My sticky note, the picture of the Nile River with its spiraling currents—they are my stones of remembrance, markers that remind me that God who was faithful before will certainly be faithful again.

*Lord, Your goodness is astounding! We call to mind Your past faithfulness, and we trust in Your future faithfulness. You have been so good to us, Lord. Would You remind us often of the ways that You have provided for us, the ways that You have come through for Your people, time and again? We ask that our trust in You would increase as we receive Your provision each day and that we would live held in Your perfect peace. Thank You, Lord. Amen.*

# 12

COME AS YOU ARE

*Practice 4: Learning to Lament*

My soul is in deep anguish.
How long, LORD, how long?

—PSALM 6:3

If you are anything like me, the practice of remembering can bring up a lot of emotion. And that is all right. While my usual take-away from times of remembrance is much like Samuel's—"Thus far the LORD has helped us"[1]—often some sadness is mixed in too. There are ways I thought the Lord might meet us, and it turns out He had different plans. There are dreams I've had to let go of. There are situations where I haven't exactly seen His provision *yet*. Can we say that the Lord has carried us and also say that we wish things might have turned out a different way?

What if remembering comes with a sting?

First and foremost, going back to His Word and prayer, picking an aspect of His character and talking to Him about it, helps center our hearts. But also, bringing that honest emotion to God instead of burying it will help us trust Him more deeply.

It's my observation that most of us in our current culture are not very good at a practice that the Israelites wove into their every day:

lament. Somewhere along the line, we have been taught that certain emotions are negative: sadness, anger, grief.

I'll be the first to say, I don't like these emotions and am often quick to run away from them. I've got all kinds of coping mechanisms, and I bet you do too. Grief is painful, and I don't like pain, so I try my best to avoid it. I keep myself busy; I work or scroll on my phone to keep my mind distracted. In my pride, I pretend that I am above grief or sadness. I bury it.

But I am learning that when I refuse to lament, I am missing an opportunity to *worship*. And I am missing an opportunity to relate with God. When we look at the book of Psalms, we see that the psalmists didn't have any notion of lament, celebration, and worship as separate things. A psalm, which was often a song to the Lord, might begin with deep grief and anguish and end in praise of God's character or celebration of all He has done. David, the writer of many psalms, frequently goes back and forth with praising God, grieving his circumstances in deep anguish, remembering who God is, crying out for help, and then celebrating all over again!

In Psalm 13, for example, we read,

How long, LORD? Will you forget me forever?
　　How long will you hide your face from me?
How long must I wrestle with my thoughts
　　and day after day have sorrow in my heart? . . .
But I trust in your unfailing love;
　　my heart rejoices in your salvation.
I will sing the LORD's praise,
　　for he has been good to me.[2]

The psalmist here both acknowledges his excruciating pain and *trusts the good and loving character of God.* Friend, grief doesn't exclude joy. Both exist together. God is faithful and life is difficult. Life is beautiful and worthy of celebration, and it is also hard and worthy of lament. And acknowledging both realities leads us to His feet.

In Uganda, my team and I work with children who have come from extraordinarily difficult situations and lived through things no child should even know of. For some of them, adults have not dependably been safe people, especially adults who are strangers, so teaching these children that they can trust us presents a significant challenge. We engage these students in all kinds of activities centered on building trust, connection, and relationship.

One simple yet powerful activity starts with a small group of children. The group leader asks a child if they would be willing to share with the group about a hurt that they have. Often the child mentions something simple or physical: "I have a paper cut" or "I fell down yesterday." The group leader, or sometimes another student in the group, then asks the child if they can put a bandage on the hurt. It is a simple illustration, and it uses a lot of bandages. But over time, it goes a long way to help children model trust in and care for others.

Eventually, the hurts they share move from small physical wounds to deep heart wounds. They get to choose if they want to wear their bandage over their heart or on their hands or feet. Slowly, they learn that they can trust their leader. And they discover this by bringing their hurt and their hard *to* their leader and allowing the hurt to be bandaged.

Isaiah says about Jesus that He comes to "bind up the brokenhearted."[3] But I suspect you and I often miss out on His compassionate healing because we're reluctant to reveal our broken parts, to admit we're in need of some serious bandaging.

If we're to succeed in our search for peace, in our commitment to surrender and trust, *we need to bring our grief to Him.*

For years before I was married, I spent time many evenings in my bathroom, one of the only quiet places in my house, even after bedtime, as babies slept in my room and bigger children liked to need *many* glasses of water. After everyone was safely tucked in bed and the tasks of the day were done, I would tiptoe back to the bathroom, take a seat, and pour out my heart and my tears, my hopes, my dreams, and my bitter disappointments before the Lord. As I think back, I can't remember exactly everything I told Him. I can't remember all the hurts and hard that I talked to Him about. What I do remember: *He was near.*

*He draws close to us as we bring our grief to Him.*

As I sat on the cold tile in those early years of parenting and ministry, I felt deep anguish. But as I think back on those times, I remember them fondly. The pain I felt is just a shadow now, and the memory that sticks is that God was with me. I learned His character on those nights in ways I would have missed if I hadn't brought my hurt to Him. I may not have known it, but I was practicing trust by being honest with my Father.

After I got married, we moved to a house with a smaller bathroom, things got busy, and, honestly, things were going okay. We had babies, and they had strange sleep schedules, and the bathroom floor became much less frequented. But over the years, I have still found myself there in times of desperation, both after the little ones are tucked in and in the middle of the day, to call out to Jesus for help.

I've realized, though, that I tend to wait to bring my grief to the Lord until I feel absolutely desperate. Something in me sees sadness or lament as weakness, when in fact it is another way to trust my Father. The first thought to fill my mind as I sit alone with my grief is often *Why am I so broken? What's wrong with me?* But recently it has been followed quickly with another realization: To know God as the God of tender mercies requires me to be in need of, desperate for, His mercy. The problem is, sometimes being needy feels whiny to me, and I really don't like whining. When things hurt deep, I tell myself that I must push onward. I will rise above. I will overcome. I tell myself things I know to be true: God is good. God is faithful. We have so much to be thankful for.

*These things are all true.* But they can be true *and* I can be sad. I can acknowledge God's goodness and not gloss over the fact that the last years have been hard. I can have questions. I can feel lonely. And I can run to God instead of away from Him, even as I feel these things.

⌣

AT THE BEGINNING of the year, I studied the book of Job. Job is called by God Himself "blameless and upright,"[4] God's faithful servant. Often as I read his story, though, I would ask Benji, who isn't just my husband but was also my pastor for many years, "Job is supposed to be righteous, right? Is he allowed to be speaking this way to God?"

If you are unfamiliar with the story, Job is an honorable man who loves the Lord and his family, seeks God's forgiveness for his transgressions and even the possible transgressions of his children, and lives in the favor of God. In short: Job is a good guy. Even so, with God's permission, Satan inflicts all kinds of hardship on Job. He destroys Job's home, his flocks, even his family. Job is plagued with painful illness and filled with grief over all he has lost. In the midst of his immense suffering, Job calls out to God, asking Him endless questions. He asks God "Why?" over and over, just like Gideon did.

Job was more honest with his suffering and his questions to God than I was comfortable with. To me, because I have been trained that sadness equals weakness and I should bury my grief, sometimes it sounded like Job was whining, complaining, even questioning God and His sovereignty and authority. Benji pointed out that even while Job questioned why God would allow such suffering, he never questioned His character. Job trusted Him enough to be gut-wrenchingly honest. It was as if Job scooted right up next to God and poured out his heart and his questions and his sadness and grief. And how does God respond?

God doesn't push Job away when he laments his hurt or when he asks God questions or even when he rails against Him in anger. God listens to Job, responds to Job, tells Job of His majesty and assures him that evil and suffering will not have the final say. He makes it very clear that, unlike what Job's friends believe, suffering *isn't* always a punishment for sin. This suffering is allowing Job to experience God in a new way, to know Him more intimately than he did before.

God doesn't answer all Job's questions. In fact, a great many of them remain unanswered. But as Job passionately expresses his deep sorrow, *God draws near* and says, "Remember who I am." Job 38:1 says that God speaks to Job out of the storm. Among many other things, God gives Job these reminders:

- *I am the God who laid the earth's foundations.*[5]
- *I am the God who gives orders to the morning, who shows the dawn its place.*[6]
- *I am the God who stores snow in storehouses, who disperses the lightning and controls the wind.*[7]
- *I am the God who satisfies the wastelands and makes the grass spring forth.*[8]

God doesn't ever give Job a reason for his suffering; He simply reminds Job of who He is, the God who is mighty and holds the whole earth in His hands.

I used to live under this assumption that all suffering would eventually resolve and end well, that I would always be able to look back and see all the good God brought out of the hard. Sometimes this is true. Sometimes it isn't. Sometimes we are stuck in the middle of the hard and the suffering and can't see the good and we don't have an answer. We feel sad and hurt and confused and we can't make sense of any of it. A voice in our head says, "I can't possibly tell God about this. Then He will know that sometimes I don't trust Him."

I chuckled as I typed that. Of course He knows. So why do I think I should bury my disappointment, my confusion, or my sadness? Maybe I think I need to protect God's character. When a loved one is hurting and the situation isn't resolving, when a loved one is sick and the healing I have prayed and cried out for just isn't coming through, when I walk alongside my friends as they face joblessness, homelessness, famine, even death, do I shy away from grief because I fear that feeling all my sadness might indicate that God has failed?

Job knows, as do David and the other psalmists, that God is so much bigger and stronger than that. My disappointment or sadness or questions or rage don't change who God is, who He has always been, who He always will be.

⌣

I WAS SO deeply grieved when we made the move from our home in Uganda to the United States. Looking back now, I know that my emotions were abundantly reasonable. We had left our home, our community, all our comforts, and everything familiar. We had left a life we loved. But often, I wouldn't let myself feel sad. God had given us *so* much as we transitioned to our temporary home in the United States. He had helped us find a great rental house, provided us with everything necessary to fill it, with schools for our children, time with our loved ones. In so many ways, He had given us everything we could need. I actually was sad, but it felt whiny to say it. It felt ungrateful.

As I thought about trust, though, as I thought about not just *saying* but actually *believing* that God was trustworthy, I realized that the people I trust most are the ones I can be most vulnerable with.

The ones who have seen me at my absolute worst and keep showing up for me. I thought about the exercise we do with our students and the bandages, teaching them that we are a safe place to bring their hurt. Would I ever push my baby away or chide him for being upset if he fell and skinned his knee and then ran to me? No! I would scoop him up and cuddle and kiss him. I would wipe away his tears.

Just like for the infant who learns to trust her caregiver by repeatedly crying and having her needs met, this is how our hearts learn to trust and attach to God. We bring Him our hurt, over and over and over again. And each time, He meets us. He loves us. He tenderly binds up our wounds and reminds us of who He is so we can always look back and say, *He was near. He was Immanuel.*

A friend and I were talking about grief recently. She and her family are walking through an impossibly hard season, and the end does not seem to be in sight. She confessed that she wonders often if God is dishonored by the fact that she has not healed and moved on yet. I looked at my friend, who has walked so faithfully through so much hurt and loss, and I could see only that God was deeply honored that she kept going back to Him when it might have felt easier to turn away. I know that He is not upset with her for not being able to "move on" and that He longs to hold her as she continues to walk this hard path. Even being aware of this, I also often subconsciously feel that I have to put on a happy face when I go to Him.

I have a tendency to "clean things up"—what I mean is that I can minimize my hurts before bringing them to God. I don't know about you, but for me it often feels hard to speak about my pain or the hardship my family experiences because so many around me suffer more than I do. I recognize that we are incredibly fortunate, that God has blessed us with profound joy and love, and I really am grateful. I also thoroughly enjoy serving others who are experiencing times of pain and suffering and am often too headstrong to acknowledge my own. Somewhere along the way, I absorbed the misguided message, much like my friend, much like many of us, that a "good Christian" should be only grateful and never complain. As a result, I wasn't trusting God with all my emotions, nor was I trusting Him to solve

## DRAW NEAR TO GOD IN YOUR GRIEF

Maybe this is all new for you and you are wondering where to begin. Maybe you have experienced seasons where you bring your honest emotions to the Lord but have fallen out of the habit, prone to the temptation to wrap everything up nicely and bring neat, tidy prayers to the Lord.

So how do you learn to lament?

First, take an honest assessment of where you are. Are there things in your life that you are grieving, wounds that are hurting, or questions you have for God that you are stuffing instead of asking because you are not sure that you are supposed to ask? Spend some time honestly revealing these things to the Lord. There is nothing He doesn't already know, but bringing it to Him will increase your trust in Him to hold it.

I want to lean in close and assure you that it is all right if you are sad about the prayers that seem unanswered, about the things in your life that aren't going the way you had planned or hoped or imagined. You can grieve the losses, even if your loss is something that hasn't happened yet, something that might not happen the way you hope. This is all part of surrender.

Jesus quotes Psalm 22 on the cross, just before He goes to His death. Spend time reading this psalm and others, noting the honest emotion and the juxtaposition of joy and grief.

Remember, "the LORD is close to the brokenhearted and saves

or sort out whatever pain I was facing. In just pushing through, I had learned to minimize my pain as not important enough to bring to Him.

those who are crushed in spirit."[17] What is breaking your heart today, friend? Can you tell our loving Father about it and believe that not only does He love you no less, but He is pleased to lovingly embrace you in all of your hurts and questions?

Find a quiet spot. I'm clearly partial to the bathroom floor, but a closet or the car in the school pickup line or an empty cubicle will work too. Allow God to remind you of who He is. Here is some help getting started:

- God is love, and we are always His beloved.[18]
- God is the God of compassion and mercy, filled with unfailing love and faithfulness.[19]
- God never changes His character; He is the same yesterday, today, and forever.[20]
- The Lord is righteous in all His ways and kind in all His works.[21]
- The Lord is trustworthy. He will do what He promises. He will remain faithful.[22]

Scripture is filled with evidence of the trustworthy character of God, and I encourage you to dive in and find some that you can add to this list.

The grief will lessen one day. Maybe it will pass completely. Maybe we will look back and see what God was doing, and maybe not. But if we allow Him to enter in, we will always look back and see that He was near and, above all, He was trustworthy. As we breathe in this new trust, we will exhale deep peace.

I wonder if you have experienced this. Have you felt that your pain isn't big enough or important enough for God? Have you felt that sharing your honest hurts and struggles would cause you to appear whiny or ungrateful in the eyes of your Father? If so, I want to assure you that you can believe in His character and still pour out your sadness, regret, disappointment, and questions. Can you pause and examine your heart to see if there are places where you have resisted being honest with God? Maybe, like the friend I sat across from last week, you have thought He would be dishonored by your sadness or disappointment that He did not show up the way you wanted or did not resolve a situation the way you had hoped.

Denying our pain and putting on a happy face for the world and for God only increases our *merimna* anxiety. What could pull us apart more than stuffing down our sadness and grief and pretending to be fine when we are not? We already know that God sees our thoughts and knows our hearts, so pretending to feel or think anything other than our honest emotions only pulls us apart and further separates us from Him.

⁓

IF GOD IS trustworthy, we can show Him that we trust Him by going to Him honestly with our emotions, doubts, questions, and fears. That doesn't cause Him to love us less but will cause *us* to love *Him* more. Just as in any human relationship, true honesty and vulnerability increase our trust and draw us closer to our Father, the only place we can experience true shalom, life-giving wholeness.

It has taken me years to understand that it's not so terrible to sometimes have doubts. So many of our biblical heroes—Moses and David and Job and Peter and even Paul—doubted sometimes. It's what we do with our doubts, our questions, our disappointment, that matters. When we don't give our doubts to God, they drive a wedge into our relationship, causing us to move further away from Him, whether intentionally or not. By contrast, I heard it said once that when we bring our doubts *to* the Lord, they drive us deeper into relationship *with* Him. That is what I have experienced in my most difficult seasons, what Jacob and Gideon and Job and David and people throughout all of history experienced as they brought their questions to God.

I don't know about you, but I am honored when a friend comes to me honestly with her sadness and brokenheartedness. When she shares the real things going on in her heart, the deep hard, the ways that she is wrestling. The first time this happens in a relationship, I think, *I'm in. She trusts me enough to bring me the real stuff.*

Lament to God is a biblical practice and, seemingly, something of a lost art, one we need to relearn.

David lamented to the Lord loudly, honestly, and often. God called David "a man after his own heart,"[9] and this wasn't because David's life choices were always pleasing to Him. But David's heart was *honest* with God—in joy and in sorrow, in victory and in deep remorse. Even when David's pain and suffering was a consequence of atrocious sin in his life, he brought his regret and sadness honestly to God.

I am often taken aback by how direct and gut-wrenchingly honest David is. He isn't trying to hide his pain from God. He isn't trying to just push through in his own strength. When he feels defeated, he lies on the floor and tells God about it. When he doesn't understand what God is up to, he lets Him know it. David, like Gideon, like Job, has big questions for God. David asks God what He is doing and why. David's heart offered bare before God as his Father, savior, and confidant is a beautiful sacrifice.

Is this okay? Can I praise God and feel thankful and grieve and lament all at the same time? Why do I think that God is going to be offended? Like Adam and Eve, I'd rather run and hide until I have my hurt and confusion packed neatly away. But the Psalms and my own past experience remind me that God, who holds all of it, has room for it all: praise and lament, thanksgiving and sorrow, all of it wrapped up together, all of it safe in His loving hands.

Listen to the words of David, similar to so many he penned.

Have mercy on me, LORD, for I am faint;
   heal me, LORD, for my bones are in agony.
My soul is in deep anguish.
   How long, LORD, how long?

Turn, LORD, and deliver me;
   save me because of your unfailing love.[10]

God saves us because of His great love for us! And because of His great love for us, He wants us to bring our questions, our doubts, and our hurts to Him.

Jesus Himself often quoted the psalms of lament. He cried out to God from the depths of His agony. And I have to believe that since Jesus is both fully man (fully experiencing the same deep pain we experience) and fully God (one with Him and fully informed of His thoughts, plans, and ways), He knew that His agony wouldn't last and would ultimately be for good. *Still,* He voiced these intimate prayers, prayers that would have been familiar to His Hebrew audience as songs of grief. Was Jesus modeling for them and for us a language to give voice to our honest heart cries and lead us to renewed trust in God?

We are conditioned from the time we are little to pick just one emotion that we are feeling at a time. We believe we can hold either grief *or* hope, sadness *or* joy. One or the other. But Jesus shows the error in that perspective. Jesus cries out to the Father in great agony, "Take this cup from me."[11] He truly dreads going to the cross; He is deeply grieved. At the same time, we read in Scripture that Jesus goes to the cross for *joy*.[12] It is His joy to obey the Father. Jesus holds both grief and joy. David holds both sorrow and praise. Job holds both deep questions and deep trust in God's character. *So can we.*

We don't have to be crushed by our grief, because as we bring it honestly to our loving Father, we will see that it does not consume us. As Paul says, "We are hard pressed . . . but not crushed; persecuted, but not abandoned; struck down, but not destroyed."[13] When we turn toward God in our grief, we can rejoice even in our deepest pain. Even here, we are seen and known and loved. We are safe.[14]

In her own beautiful book about peace, Morgan Harper Nichols wrote, "May we learn to be less afraid of the shadows. And may we realize that just because they are a part of the picture, that doesn't mean that's all there is."[15] There is hard, but there isn't only hard. There is sadness, but there isn't only sadness. There are morning cappuccinos and baby giggles and sunsets too. And the shadows are a lot less scary when we invite Jesus into them instead of pretending they aren't there at all.

IN RECENT MONTHS, I have begun to name all my deep hurt and loss and tell it to God. I told Him I was confused. I told Him I was tired. I told Him that I didn't want to always revert back to controlling and managing and running. He already knows it all, so it's pretty silly to hide it anyway. I would never be able to stop worrying about future pain until I gave my unhealed wounds to Him. I knew that God could see the grief in my heart no matter how far I buried it and that, just like with Job, He might not tell me why He had allowed certain hardships but He would remind me of who He is.

I think of Job and I think of David and I think of Jesus, who, in His darkest hour, cries out to His Father, "My God, my God, why have you forsaken me?"[16] It is okay for us to cry out to the Lord and lay our honest questions before Him. *What is happening here, God? Why?* Maybe He will answer us. Maybe He will deliver us from our suffering. Maybe He will reveal a new aspect of His character to us. *Always,* He will be with us in it.

We are allowed to hurt. In the presence of our gracious Father, all our messy, gritty feelings are okay. When we bring our honest feelings to the Lord, when we cry out to Him, we are practicing biblical lament, acknowledging that the world around us is broken, hard, often terrible even.

We must speak the reality of our grief to God, not because He doesn't already know but because when we tell Him, we are also saying that we believe He cares, that we believe He can do something about it. We say, *Lord, I don't understand this, but I trust You with it.* Lament cries out to God to deliver us from our pain or meet us in our pain. And the more we practice, the more God proves Himself trustworthy. The more we lament to Him honestly and allow Him to meet us, the more stones of remembrance we have in our arsenal, the more we can trust, the more His deep and abiding peace settles down over our hearts.

When we go to God with our real emotions, with our deep grief and our suffering and our questions, we proclaim that we have a God who hears us, a God who sees us, a God who does not turn away from the hurting. He is not a passive or distant God but Immanuel, God who is with us even in our darkest times.

*Lord, we confess our tendency to "clean things up" before we come to You, attempting to conceal our sin or grief. In truth, we know that nothing is hidden from You. We thank You that You see all our emotions, all our wrestling, even all our sadness, and You love us anyway. We praise You that You are*

*God, who can handle all of us, all our feelings. Lord, we ask that You would teach us to lament and that our laments would lead us back to praise, back to a place of trust and peace. Thank You for holding us close as we hurt. We love You. Amen.*

# 13

# WORSHIP ALONG THE WAY

*Practice 5: Training Our Hearts to Praise*

The LORD is good to those whose hope is in him,
to the one who seeks him.

—LAMENTATIONS 3:25

If you flip through the book of Psalms in your Bible, you will find plenty of lament passages. But as we saw in the previous chapter, it's vital to note that the Psalms are not just lament and questions; they are lament and *praise*.

Let's look again at Psalm 13:

How long, LORD? Will you forget me forever?
How long will you hide your face from me?
How long must I wrestle with my thoughts
and day after day have sorrow in my heart? . . .
But I trust in your unfailing love;
my heart rejoices in your salvation.
I will sing the LORD's praise,
for he has been good to me.[1]

Even as David voices his complaints and doubts to the Lord about his current situation, even as he wonders if God has forsaken him, even as he remembers his grief and affliction, he continues to praise God for who He is. Lament and remembering should always lead us back to worship.

I love pretty much any words from John Piper, but I've held on to these, especially over the past season: "Occasionally weep deeply over the life you hoped would be. Grieve the losses. Then wash your face. Trust God. And embrace the life you have."[2]

It's okay to be sad, it's okay to lament, but it's not okay to stay there forever. Lament. Grieve. Cry out. And then turn your heart back to praise. Not because you have everything you want. Not because the circumstance has changed. Not because things are necessarily going your way. But because you can trust in God's unfailing love and because, in Jesus, He has been good to us. No matter what is happening around you, God remains worthy of your worship.

When you are in the book of Psalms, you will see a section of them, each with the label "A Song of Ascents." These are the songs Israelites committed to memory and would sing as they climbed up Mount Zion on their way to worship in Jerusalem.

Doing this was their worship for the journey, their worship in the middle, their worship *on the way*. As they climbed the treacherous mountains, sometimes going without food and water, sleeping along roadsides and relying on the kindness of strangers, they sang. Far from home and all things familiar, without amenities or comforts, they sang. They sang praises, remembering who their God was and would continue to be, even while they were still climbing.

Sure, it feels easy to praise God when things are going well, when we are on the proverbial mountaintop. When we can see the view from above and realize that we were always safe. But the Psalms teach us that we can worship Him on the way. When things are not yet resolved, when we might not *feel* worshipful, when everything still feels like a bit of a mess, we can train our hearts to praise.

In my own life, it happens that, just as Scripture I have hidden away often surfaces in times of anxiety, a worship song sometimes drops into my heart and rises to my lips right when I am beginning to feel the weight of being most desperate and downtrodden. For years and years, when I have found myself alone in the dark, rocking a sick child back to sleep, praying over a dying friend, sitting alone in the bathroom, in the car, in the back of the sanctuary, nursing an infant in the middle of the night, one particular old hymn comes to mind that starts, "I love you, Lord, and I lift my voice."[3] I have sung it over all my children as they slept, and I hum it now as I type. That is what David experiences as he laments and turns toward God. That is what the Israelites experience as they worship in the wilderness. Worship rises in the dark. *Oh, my soul, rejoice!*

Once I push aside my coping mechanism of control and lay my grief at the feet of tender Jesus, though it doesn't disappear entirely, it gets lighter. Grief takes up a little less space, which leaves space for something else. *For joy.* As we surrender our anxieties and our worries, our fear and our burdens, to Jesus, as we cry out in our suffering and hurt, He alone can change our mourning into dancing.[4]

THE MIDDLE OF Acts 16 finds Paul and Silas in prison. They have been slandered for healing a woman of an evil spirit and then publicly stripped, beaten with rods, flogged, and thrown into prison, where their feet were fastened with shackles. And in the middle of the night, Paul and Silas decide to worship. They pray aloud and sing hymns to God in the hearing of the other prisoners. Even on the hardest days, they know the joy of the Cross and the Resurrection.

"Suddenly there was such a violent earthquake that the foundations of the prison were shaken. At once all the prison doors flew open, and everyone's chains came loose."[5]

*Worship* broke their chains.

*Worship* shook the prison.

*Worship* opened the doors and set them free.

And that very night, the jailer and his whole family believed in Jesus and rejoiced.[6]

I can't tell you how many times a familiar worship song has been my lifeline on a difficult day, in a difficult season. My children often tire of me playing the same songs over and over again, but my heart needs to internalize the words until they become second nature, until my mind believes them. Even on my darkest days, nothing and no one can take from me the hope and comfort that come from my salvation, the joy that comes from knowing God, who loves me!

I'll be the first to admit in this recent season of deferred dreams and great uncertainty that being joyful hasn't exactly been my MO. I've heard myself say things like "I just don't like it here" and "I wish we were somewhere else." And while these sentiments carry some truth, they also point to an internal pity party that is ugly and robbing me and anyone around me of the joy that God would love to give me in this season and in every season.

Our grief can be holy when we bring it honestly to Jesus, but when it turns to complaining and self-pity, it becomes a dangerous weapon of the Enemy. Remember the statistic I shared earlier, that it takes our brains three seconds to encode a memory of shame but sixty to ninety seconds to encode joy? That means that choosing joy might be hard work sometimes. That means that living in the joy of our salvation even in the midst of the hard is going to take practice.

I want to take a minute to ask you about this honestly because I need my friends to do this for me. Are there places in your life where you have moved past lament into all-out self-pity? Have you been stuck wishing away your circumstances, bemoaning your current situation? If so, don't spin into shame over it (we've all been there), but hear me lovingly say that it's time to wash your face. It's time to pull out a song of ascents and worship God, even in the middle of the journey, even when you are still on the way. What can you rejoice in here and now, even if your situation or circumstance isn't what you had hoped it would be?

God, who loves you, made a way for you to have relationship with Him, now and in eternity. That is always a reason to rejoice. He is worthy of our praise.

Worship might be the very thing that begins to shake us out of our prisons of self-pity. Worship might be the very thing that begins to loosen the chains that bind us with shame and guilt and worry. Worship might be the very thing to set us free, to lead us into peace. And when others see us worshipping in the dark, it might be the very thing that would point them to Jesus.

Turn on the music, beloved. Play that same song over and over if you have to. Hum it while you drive and while you fold the laundry and while you rock the baby to sleep. We are called to be a joyful people because we know the God of Joy.

⁓

FOR YEARS, THE screen saver on my phone has been these words of Jeremiah from the book of Lamentations:

This I call to mind
    and therefore I have *hope:*

Because of the LORD's great love we are not consumed,
    for his compassions never fail.
They are new every morning;
    great is your faithfulness.[7]

What sweet words for seasons when we have to fight to trust Him, minute by minute, morning by morning. Jeremiah continues,

I say to myself, "The LORD is my portion;
    therefore I will wait for him."


The LORD is good to those whose hope is in him,
    to the one who seeks him;
it is good to wait quietly
    for the salvation of the LORD.[8]


*When we can't rejoice in anything else, we can always rejoice in the truth of who God is.*

I love these words because they are beautiful and comforting. Because over and over in my life, I have known these words to be true—that His compassion doesn't ever fail, that His mercy is new again and again. But there is something I love about these words even more that stopped me in my tracks when I first realized it, and it is the context in which they were written. Lamentations is, as you might assume by the title, *not* a book of rejoicing; it is one giant lament, a letter of grief and weeping to the Lord.

Remember how we built trust with our students by having them tell us their hurts and then allowing us to bandage them? That is what Jeremiah is doing in Lamentations. He is bringing all his pain and sorrow before the Lord.

Jeremiah is devastated by the destruction all around him. God's chosen people have refused over and over to turn back to God. Just earlier in the same passage, Jeremiah writes, "I am the man who has seen affliction. . . . [God] made me walk in darkness . . . and left me without help. . . . I remember my affliction and my wandering, the bitterness."[9] Jeremiah is in pain. He is sad, heartbroken even.

And one little word shifts everything: *yet.*

Jeremiah shifts his gaze. He calls to mind the great truths of the Lord, and they give him hope. When he cannot rejoice in his circumstances, when he cannot see anything good up ahead, he can rejoice in who God is. *Because of His great love, we are not consumed. Great is His faithfulness.* When everything else looks bleak, He is faithful and we are beloved. Nothing in Jeremiah's situation changes before he says "yet."[10] Jerusalem is still destroyed. God's people are still devastated. Jeremiah is still suffering immensely. *The only thing that changes in the midst of his suffering is the posture of his heart.*

Instead of choosing to focus on all that God hasn't done for him, he chooses to remember *who God is.* Jeremiah *chooses joy* when his circumstances are not joyful. I can too. I must.

This is a strange kindness of God in the midst of our suffering. When my situation and my circumstances are good, when I have everything I need and more, joy and celebration seem easy. I can find contentment in the good gifts God is giving me. But when things around me fall apart, when I don't have what I need (or at least what I think I need), when the waters rise and the rapids swirl, true joy and contentment can be found only in the Giver.

After explaining to His disciples that He will suffer and die, Jesus says in John 15:11, "I have told you this so that my joy may be in you and that your joy may be complete." When we know Jesus, our joy doesn't come from our outward circumstances or the things He has (or hasn't) given us; it comes from our salvation. Even on the hardest days, we have the Cross and the Resurrection. Even on the darkest days, we can find our joy in Him.

⌒

THE PRACTICE OF thanksgiving has been my saving grace more than once in all kinds of seasons, a way to shift my focus from self-pity to the goodness and grace of God. Thanksgiving is my "yet."

Sometimes it's been lists of things I am grateful for on sticky notes all over the kitchen. (I know. I have this thing for sticky notes. They are just so handy.) Sometimes a journal, listing my thanks, has lain open on the counter, an idea inspired by my friend Ann Vos-kamp's courageous book *One Thousand Gifts*. Sometimes my thanks-giving has been whispered prayers of feeble gratitude. Sometimes it has been singing the tune to a favorite worship song when my heart felt far from worshipful.

When I realized how joyless I had become during our first few months of transition, I pulled out a journal and started making a list of thanksgiving once again:

1. A house to live in
2. A cozy couch
3. Unlikely laughter
4. Picture books in the sunshine
5. Joy in this unexpected place

I listed the things big and small that He had given in this season. Honestly, some days it felt really hard, but I made it my discipline to add something to the list each day. Slowly and steadily, my heart pos-ture began to shift. I didn't really like it here . . . yet. I didn't really know what we were doing here . . . yet. I didn't see the deep healing I was hoping for . . . yet. I didn't see the restored relationships I'd been praying about for years . . . yet.

*Yet* I have hope in a savior who is coming back to restore all things. Yet I can take joy in His nearness. Yet I can have deep peace because my trials lead to steadfastness, because even in the darkest night and the biggest storms, Jesus is in the boat with us. Yet even in the deepest hurts, regret, waiting, and sorrow, God sees the whole path and will, in fact, bring us through.

I was retraining my brain for joy. I was replacing my stress, frus-tration, and anxiety with the peace Jesus promised. This was my song of ascents.

Helen Keller said that there is joy in self-forgetfulness.[11] And isn't it true? As I turn my eyes away from myself, away from my own troubles, my own shattered expectations and disappointments and deep hurts, and focus them on the Creator and His good gifts, there is such awe, such gratitude, such adoration, that I am surprised by joy, undone with joy.

Jeremiah had a great hope, an almost rebellious hope, a hope that looked at the world around him and said, *This is bad, but God is good.* And God will give good, God will bring good, even when we don't see it yet. I want this hope, this resolute rejoicing.

During our recent move, it became more apparent to me than ever that I am tempted to find my joy in my circumstances and in

## THOUGHT EXCHANGE

How do we practice joy when our circumstances aren't what we had hoped, when *we* aren't what we had hoped, when life seems to crumble?

First, we remember that *the Lord is near.* No matter how far you feel from Him, He is Immanuel, God with us.

Then, we surrender again our control, our grief, our fears, our loss, and we replace these things with conversation with God, telling Him how we feel, asking Him for what we need. As Paul says in Philippians, we replace our anxious thoughts with prayer, petition, and thanksgiving. We worship because of who God is, regardless of our feelings or our circumstances.

What are you anxious about today? What do you want God to do? What are you asking or petitioning Him for? Find a quiet place and say those things out loud to God. Maybe get on your things (good gifts from God) instead of finding my true joy in God, the Giver of all gifts, the Giver of the greatest gift: salvation in Jesus.

This helps me shift my thoughts. When I am celebrating and joyful, I ask myself where the joy is coming from—the gifts or the Giver—and I ask God to allow me to remember and hold on to this same joy in seasons of lack or hardship. When I am grieving and not feeling joyful, the same applies: I ask Him to remind me that He is the Giver of all good things and the Giver of my salvation and joy no matter what is going on around me.

When the world seems impossibly chaotic, in the midst of a family crisis or in the day-to-day mundane when our prayers go unan-

---

knees or open your hands so that your physical body is in a posture of surrender too. Now let's fill that space created by surrender with thanksgiving. Make a list of things that you are thankful for. Name them out loud to God, or write them down and keep that list going. Even if you run out of gifts to count, you can always rejoice in the Giver of salvation.

Sing your favorite worship song, or borrow mine from earlier: "I Love You, Lord." Worship of our savior pushes back the darkness and reminds us of an eternity that is certain, a joy that will never be taken away.

After Moses and the Israelites look back out over the sea, they sing.[19] There are desert paths and winding roads and gory battles up ahead, yet they can sing. They can rejoice. "The LORD is my strength and my song, and he has become my salvation."[20]

That is always reason enough to rejoice.

swered and God feels distant, can we remember who He is? Can we remember His great love for us, His great faithfulness, and His compassions that *never fail*? When life is not what we had hoped, can we declare that Jesus is still enough? Can you say, "The Lord is my portion, and I will wait for Him"? Rejoicing is a form of worship, and worship will break our chains.

$$\backsim$$

"YOU WILL GO out in joy and be led forth in peace," God promises through the prophet Isaiah.[12] *God promises.* The Israelites sing their songs of ascents not when they reach the top but on their way there.

Are you headed into the deep waters of trial or suffering, friend? Or maybe you are already neck-deep. What might it look like in your own life to anticipate God's presence there with you, to eagerly expect what He can and might do and to rejoice now, not just on the other side? What would it look like to begin to rejoice along the way, knowing that the Deliverer Himself walks with you, rather than waiting to celebrate after deliverance arrives?

When we feel a true peace that God holds the future, when we know His goodness in the deepest parts of ourselves, this goodness that we have seen when we bring our grief to Him, when we truly trust Him with our whole hearts, with all the things that are most important to us, leaning not on our own understanding, *joy is the only possible outcome.*

It may feel strange or foreign or rebellious to choose joy in a world that is upside down. But if God is who He says He is, we have no choice but to rejoice. To hope. And this rejoicing leads us into peace.

Simply because of God's loving presence, joy can be found in the hardest places. But we have to choose to see it. Sometimes we are so focused on our misery that we are blinded to what is right in front of us.

The middle of Genesis 21 finds Hagar and her son, Ishmael, in the desert. When the water in her waterskin is gone, Hagar leaves her son in the shade of a bush and walks around the corner because she cannot bear to watch her son die. As she sits down, she begins to sob. But God hears her crying and opens her eyes and she sees a well of water. Scripture doesn't say God made a new well appear; it says He opened Hagar's eyes to see it. And then just a short walk away, she filled up her waterskin with water for her son.[13]

Is it possible that in her pain and despair, Hagar assumes the worst—that God is not with her, that He will not help her, that He does not see her suffering—and that this perspective is what blinds her to the well in front of her?

Is it possible that in my own trials or pain, I let that same lie sneak in—that God couldn't possibly see me, that maybe this time He has left me or maybe this time will be the time that He does not come to my aid—and my eyes become so fixed on that lie that I am blinded to the grace and joy right in front of me, all around me, or perhaps just around the corner?

I need Him to open my eyes.

As I dug through some of my old journals recently, I found a crumpled piece of paper in the back of a notebook, recording a very specific scene at our home in Uganda:

Nineteen people ring the table. It's too many and we don't really fit. We are a whole tangled mess of elbows and knees and "Please pass the salt," and no one can hear because everyone is talking and the laughter is too loud. And though this lump of fear and sadness sits in my throat, there is something else here too. It is joy. It rises up and surprises me.

And long after the table is cleared, I sit and I wonder. Against all odds, here we are. As life as we know it crumbles to the ground, as I wonder if all that I have spent my whole life building will indeed go up in flames, we circle this table and we grab for bread and there is joy in this place.

There is no rhyme or reason for it, no other explanation but that God just keeps pouring out and we just keep receiving, that even when we think we are empty, He won't ever let us be truly empty, because He alone fills us. And when He lives in us, this surprising, glowing ember of joy brims up, even in the darkness. Sometimes we have to fight to find it. Sometimes we can't help but let it rise in our hearts in the midst of the impossible.

I glanced at the date and realized this scrawl in black ink was written haphazardly before I fell into bed one night in the middle of my season of deepest uncertainty. And that's the thing about joy. It's right there alongside the sadness, if only we would reach out and grab hold of it.

There are stars in the dark night. There is a glass of cool water in the midst of drought. There are friends and family in seasons of deep pain. There is laughter in hospital waiting rooms and funeral homes and bomb shelters. Even in our not good, God can bring His very good. This is life, the good and the bad all rolled up together, laughter and suffering, joy and hardship. We can be sad and we can also be happy.

Beloved, the well is here. Our well is Jesus. His grace, His joy—they never run out. But we have to choose to see them. We have to ask Him to open our eyes to His goodness right here in the middle of the desert. We need His grace like Hagar and Ishmael need water. And it doesn't come from within.

Maybe you feel it too, like you are here in the wilderness with your own empty waterskin and if you don't find some grace soon, then you just won't be able to keep going. It's true. Without Him, we perish. God has to open our eyes to the well before we can drink from it. And He opens our eyes to the truth of His grace and goodness through our time in His Word, our time of remembrance, our time lamenting at His feet.

Can you say with Jeremiah, "Yet I have hope"? Can you hum that line of "I Love You, Lord" with me: "Oh, my soul, rejoice"?

AS YOU MAY know, Hagar found herself in the desert more than once. In Genesis 16, near a spring in the desert as a pregnant runaway, she encountered the angel of the Lord and declared, "You are the God who sees me."[14] He is the God who sees us, and He is the God who makes us see.

When I forget that He is the God who sees me, I am blind. But when I, like Hagar, call out to Him, remembering His grace, He gives me eyes to see Him right here in the desert. He provides the well of grace in this moment—enough for today. He provides the well of joy in all circumstances—even the hardest. He provides the well of His goodness—even in the midst of this world's pain.

In Philippians 4, Paul instructs believers to "rejoice in the Lord always."[15] It is so important that he says it again—"Rejoice!" And I used to think that I could rejoice only if I *felt* joyful and I felt joyful only if I was happy, specifically if I was happy with my outward circumstance. But since Paul is speaking to a body of believers who are facing all kinds of hardship and persecution, he simply can't be instructing them to rejoice because of how they feel or what is going on in their lives. He goes on to say, "The Lord is near. Do not be anxious about anything, but in every situation, by prayer and petition, *with thanksgiving*, present your requests to God."[16] In other words, thanksgiving is a way to put off our anxiety and embrace God's peace instead.

*The joy of God's nearness is our ticket to not being anxious.*

And here is the glorious promise: As we rejoice—as we know His nearness, as we surrender our anxieties and persistently, *with thanksgiving,* bring our prayers and requests to Him—the peace of God that transcends all understanding will guard our hearts and our minds in Christ Jesus.[17]

The peace of Jesus guards us as we turn our eyes away from our present circumstance and toward Him. As we behold Him, as we worship Him.

Jeremiah chooses joy as the world falls apart, not because he feels happy but because he knows God. The Lord is near. Hagar rejoices in the Lord when all seems impossible, and God who sees her opens her eyes to see. On the way up the mountain, the Israelites sing,

> Our mouths were filled with laughter,
>     our tongues with songs of joy.
> Then it was said among the nations,
>     "The Lord has done great things for them."
> The Lord has done great things for us,
>     and we are filled with joy. . . .
> Those who sow with tears
>     will reap with songs of joy.[18]

I want these things to be true of me too. I want to choose joy not as a feeling but as a lifestyle. I don't want to be someone who rejoices and worships only when life is good but someone who rejoices in God and worships Him for His goodness no matter what is going on. I don't want to just be thankful for the gifts; I want to rejoice in the Giver.

In this life, we may lose more than we could imagine. We may at times hurt to the point of thinking we may not survive. But with eyes on Him, we will know more joy than we dare dream.

*Father God, You call us to be people of praise, and You give us Your love, Your grace, and Your mercy to turn our hearts to worship You. Give us thankful hearts no matter the circumstance. Remind us that, in Jesus, there is always something to be grateful for. You have done great things for us; let us be filled with joy in Your presence. Even on the most difficult of days, God, give us hearts, minds, and voices to sing your praise and testify of Your goodness. Amen.*

# 14

## DWELL IN THE LAND
### *Practice 6: Practicing Presence*

Trust in the LORD and do good;
dwell in the land and enjoy safe pasture.

—PSALM 37:3

A few months before we moved from Uganda to the United States, God prompted me to plant a garden. I'd been feeling unusually angsty, as we knew a change of some kind was imminent but weren't yet sure of the timeline. I found my head spinning often with what-ifs and shoulds and shouldn'ts. Should we really go, or shouldn't we? Wouldn't it be so much easier to stay? And if we should go, when? Where? *How?* It felt like there were a million decisions to make—schools, jobs, home, ministry, timeline, church—and I wanted to have every one of them squared away and figured out perfectly before we took a single step in any direction. I spent far too much mental energy meticulously planning out the future, then making a backup plan in case those best-laid plans didn't work.

As I sit here now, on the other side of our big move, it is easy to laugh and shake my head. Exactly zero of the things I spent time agonizing over actually ended up mattering much. Things are vastly different from what I had planned or imagined, yet here we are: well provided for, surrounded by His goodness, joyful even.

But back then, I was trying to anticipate and architect a future that might never happen. When I recognized how I'd been letting my mind spin, I began to take my anxious thoughts to the Lord. I whispered Psalm 91 to myself often:

> Whoever dwells in the shelter of the Most High
>     will rest in the shadow of the Almighty.
> I will say of the LORD, "He is my refuge and my fortress,
>     my God, in whom I trust."[1]

I needed the rest this passage promised. What did it mean to *dwell*? As I asked this of the Lord, I felt the same prompting over and over again, the words dropping into my heart as if out of nowhere: *Plant a garden.*

You should know I am a notoriously bad gardener. I have always wanted to be one of those people with a beautiful, sprawling vegetable garden. I love the idea of slow days in the sunshine, harvesting homegrown veggies, working with my hands, and getting gloriously dirty alongside things that live and grow by the grace of God. I love His clear provision in gardens, everything we need in what He has already given. "Consider the lilies of the field,"[2] Jesus says.

Despite the beauty of that vision, I never actually do it. A couple of times, I have started. I've drawn out plans and saved things on Pinterest and purchased seeds. I even grew some really big eggplants once, only to realize that I didn't have enough tried-and-true recipes to put that much eggplant to use. Occasionally, I will plant something, and sometimes, while the garden is still new, I will remember to water and prune it regularly. But with life already verging on too full, the plants take a back seat to the people coming in and out of our home. Eventually, the garden ends up dead or overgrown or overrun with weeds.

During the Covid-19 lockdown, I had my most success with gardening to date. (Set your expectations low.) Being tethered to our house, I spent time making some cute garden beds. Benji bought me great fertilizer, and with very minimal effort, I grew basil, rosemary, oregano, chives, and exactly three tomatoes. Southeastern Uganda is a dream for a terrible gardener like me because the soil is so fertile and the sunshine so plentiful that things just grow wildly without much help. I was proud of my little garden, and I loved it as much as I thought I would. As the world spun out of control around me, I dug my hands deep into the black earth of my own backyard. Weeks later, my children helped me pick fresh basil, and we had fragrant herbs for sauces and soups for months to come.

Inevitably, though, the lockdown eased, and life went back to its usual, faster pace. The herb garden didn't die, really; it just got overgrown and full of weeds and we all kind of forgot about it.

Add this history to the fact that we now seemed to be on the verge of a pretty drastic move, and I wondered, *What could planting a garden even accomplish?* I kept brushing off the thought. It was probably me, not God's prompting. But in the quiet of the night, when my thoughts would spin with ideas of the future and all its uncertainty, when I would feel completely overwhelmed with the need to make the *right* decision *right* now, the gentle nudging was still there: *Plant a garden.*

As I began to pray and ask the Lord if this was, in fact, His voice, I began to discern that He might not be suggesting that I plant an actual garden with seeds. Maybe He was nudging me to dig in deeper and get into the dirt alongside other things that live and grow by His grace. In other words, people.

"Trust in the Lord and do good; dwell in the land and enjoy safe pasture," we're told in Psalm 37.³ *Maybe to dwell in the shelter of the*

*Most High is to just be.* To live in our place, to love our people, to dig our hands into the dirt of what is right in front of us, where He has already placed us. To stop racing ahead to the future or trying to mentally rewrite the past but to just be here today, receiving His goodness, trusting His care. Maybe digging in and doing good in the place that God already had me instead of fretting about where He might move us next was just another exercise in trusting Him fully.

So my five-year-old son and I planted some watermelon seeds, and I asked God to bring to mind young people in our community in need of encouragement. Even as I did, the reasonable arguments kept coming to my mind: *We might not even be here much longer. Why would I start anything now? Why would I invest in relationships only to leave them? If I pour into these kids now, I might not be here long enough to see any results.*

*Dwell in the land,* the psalmist urged. It wasn't really about the outcome. My little guy might not get to eat his watermelon, but he thoroughly loved just getting dirty and the anticipation that one day there might be watermelon. I can see now that's what I needed too. I needed to dig in deep. I needed to be *all in* exactly where He had me *right now* or my anxiety about the future would cause me to miss the beauty right in front of me. I needed to anticipate and hope again for things I could not yet see as a way to say, *God, I trust You to give good, even when I cannot see it yet.*

That week, I invited over a handful of teenage girls from our neighborhood to study the book of Psalms with me. I opened some bags of popcorn and put out a bunch of greasy samosas I had bought on my way home from town. (These flaky pastries filled with peas are readily available at roadside stands in our little Ugandan town.) I opened the Bible and read out loud things that I knew to be true but that I was often quick to forget.

And for a few hours, I stopped all my wondering and my anxious heart stilled as I taught my neighbors of the goodness of God as we laid hands on one another and prayed for one another. I looked into their eyes and I heard the cries of their hearts.

Later that evening, I weeded and pruned my herb garden.

"Delight yourself in the Lord," the psalmist continues, "and he will give you the desires of your heart."[4] I desired peace to transcend my pulled-apart thinking and planning, and God would give me that peace, that wholeness, as I focused on what was right in front of me and left the rest up to Him. As I learned to dwell in Him, He would give not just my body but my heart rest in the shadow of His wings.

If I had known we'd be leaving so soon the community we deeply adored, I never would have initiated that Bible study. Why start something you can't finish? Why plant something you won't see bloom? I thought quite the opposite, actually—that if God truly was prompting me to dig in deep here, then surely soon He would reveal to us that it wasn't time to move yet.

Oh, friend, He works in ways we can never foresee. There will always be circumstances in our lives that leave us feeling unsettled or anxious, unable to focus on the present. The future unknown beckons us to ruminate on all that might go wrong and dream about all that might go well. Maybe you are looking toward a new job, launching your child into adulthood, anticipating a move, expecting a new baby, going back to work. What is drawing your thoughts away from today and into tomorrow? How can you continue to dwell where He has you right now, resting in the shadow of His wings?

What He is showing me now in hindsight is that sometimes we need to dig our fingers into the grit and dirt of where we are for our own benefit, not for the outcome. Sometimes we need to slow down and just feel the sun on our faces and be thankful for the gift of today.

Sometimes we just need to dwell—to live fully, right where we are.

## A MOMENT'S NOTICE

How can you be more present today, this week? Take a moment to pause. Listen. Look. Feel. What is present around you? Notice your current surroundings and invite God into them. (He's already there, by the way, but this helps us remind ourselves of His presence.)

What would it look like to dwell with Him today, to give Him your swirling thoughts and emotions and stay captivated by His goodness and provision right in front of you?

If you can, go on a walk. I know it sounds simple, but we might all need it a little more than we think. Go on a walk and listen to the birds or the wind. Notice the trees and flowers. Spend some time being reminded that God, who created all this and provides for all of His creation, intends to lovingly provide you with everything you need, no matter what comes. Feel His gaze on you, loving you.

Recently, I began the practice of starting our homeschool day by reciting Psalm 118:24 out loud together:

> This is the day that the LORD has made;
> let us rejoice and be glad in it. (ESV)

Doing this is so simple, but it helps me (and hopefully my children) center our hearts on Jesus and His gift in this day. Maybe you could join us in this practice.

Whoever dwells in the shelter of the Most High
  will rest in the shadow of the Almighty.
I will say of the LORD, "He is my refuge and my fortress,
  my God, in whom I trust."[5]

Nothing says we trust God like learning to dwell, learning to be present and planted where our feet are.

For the next several Tuesdays, these young women trickled into my house. They opened up more and more, sharing things that were hard in their daily lives, things that they were struggling to believe about God or themselves. They were a great encouragement to me as they reminded me of truths that *I* was struggling to believe about God and myself. We laughed and we cried and we read and we prayed.

And just a few months later, when we did leave Uganda (at least for this season), they showed up with hugs and notes of love and encouragement. They circled around our family with arms outstretched and tears streaming as we prayed together.

*Planting is never for nothing.*

*Planting says we trust our God.*

*Planting is how we dwell.*

*Planting leads to peace.*

There is great benefit in just being fully where we are. There is great hope in pouring ourselves into right now and trusting God that fruit will come in time, whether or not we get to see or partake of it.

We make bumper stickers and T-shirts out of that famous Jim Elliot quote "Wherever you are, be all there."[6] But it is a lot easier said than done. A million things are vying for our attention: our cell phones full of other people's lives, perfectly curated to inform us of all the ways we aren't measuring up; our thoughts and dreams and fears of the future swirling in our minds; uncertainty around just about everything in the world right now; a million decisions, big and small, all of which seem pressing and urgent.

Maybe what we need is to dig our hands deep into the soil of the place that God has given us right now, today. To get dirty and sun-kissed with the people He has put in our lives at this moment. To laugh and cry and know Him alongside others grown by His grace.

I think fondly on that last season in Uganda, full of basil and Bible study on the couch and greasy snacks. Bible study and garden-ing became my refuge from the anxious thoughts that threatened to overcome me, the swirling worry the Enemy wanted to use to pull me into the future and cause me to miss today. Tending to my herbs and my local community wasn't just for their benefit but also for mine, a God-given gift of presence.

A FEW MONTHS after our relocation to the United States, I broke down in big heaving sobs while meeting with my therapist. I couldn't put my finger on why I was even crying exactly. It just all felt like too much; everything was moving too fast; everything was too hard, too different. I was drowning. Once again, my head was spinning with the what-ifs: *What if the kids don't do well here? What if we just can't adjust to this pace of life? What if we never make friends? What if we never find a church? What if this wasn't even the right decision?*

"I think you need to go to some places," she said as I looked at her questioningly. "Go see if you can find some places in this new town that you like. Touch the bricks of the buildings. Plant your feet on the ground."

There it was again—that nudging. *Plant. Dwell.* Plant here, where you are, today. Not because you know what the fruit will be, not because you know if you are here long-term or not, but because you are here *now* and you are alive and you are part of something bigger than yourself, namely, living alongside other things that live and grow by God's grace alone.

I'll admit I was stubborn about taking her advice. Four or five weeks later, I finally ventured out to find a place. I realize that I am hesitant to like this place or anything in it because it feels a bit like forsaking the other place I loved so much, as if maybe finding something I love here or settling in here would negate my immense love for our other home that we so truly adore. I don't really want to find a new coffee shop to write in because my heart still aches for the coffee shop that I used to write in, where I knew the staff and they knew my order and my kids and would let me pay them tomorrow.

But I took a big breath and drove through the November sunshine and tentatively walked into a coffee shop. I ordered a latte and snuck out to the little back patio with exposed brick walls and metal chairs and creeping vines. It all felt so far away from and yet so similar to my very favorite little coffee shop in Jinja. I took my shoes off. And when I snapped a picture of my table to show my husband the cute little nook I had found, the sun made a rainbow in my phone screen right over the table. I cried a little then because being in a new place is hard and future uncertainty is hard, but my Certain God was in that surprise rainbow and He would be in this coffee shop the way He was in the other one.

*Plant a garden,* He whispers. *Dwell here with Me, in Me.* And I am overcome by His grace to allow us to plant and sow and reap and plant again. As Morgan Harper Nichols has said, "Practicing peace is a lifelong process of coming back to the present moment over and over again."[7]

I don't know where you are today, dear one. Maybe you are enjoying, as I did for years, deep community and steadiness in a familiar place, and that is a beautiful gift and provision from the Lord. Maybe you are on the verge of something that feels big—a decision is looming and you don't know exactly which path to take. Maybe you have already made the decision and the change is imminent and you want to trust God with your future but your thoughts still race ahead and you aren't quite sure how to rein them back in. Maybe you are tempted to live in the past, kicking yourself over old regrets and mistakes. Maybe you are in a new place and you don't like it yet and you aren't sure if you ever will and wonder what to do with that. Maybe the uncertainty of the past few years has left you *exhausted*—not sleepy tired but deep-in-your-bones tired—and you can't really imagine anticipating or hoping for good things anymore.

Let me look long into your eyes and tell you that you are not alone. We have all been there at least a time or two. And let me whisper to you gently the way the Lord did to my heart: "Plant a garden." Ask Him for discernment of what that might mean in your own life and season right now. *But wherever you are, be all there. Dwell in the shelter of our Most High God. Rest with Him awhile.*

He may lead you to plant an actual, physical garden, to feel the sun on your face and the earth beneath your fingernails and exhale in His provision. He may nudge you toward a person or two whom you could really invest in or be vulnerable with. He may push you toward a new coffee shop where you will one day order your favorite drink without tearing up. (I'm not there yet.)

Today is an abundant gift God has given us, and the only day guaranteed to us. Let's practice being present and enjoying His good gifts. Let's practice putting our feet on the ground and being where we are, with our people in our place. Let's allow this to be our defiant act of trust in the Lord.

*Father, we long to be present where we are, but so often our minds race ahead to the future or get stuck in the past. We need Your help as we purpose to receive this day, this moment, as a gift. Give us this day our daily bread, God. Cause us to plant deep roots where we are right now, in this season, in this day. Cause us to dwell with You, in You. As we fix our eyes on You, may our days and even our minutes be pleasing to You. We love You. Amen.*

# 15

---

# THE BETTER THING

*Practice 7: Creating Space for Rest*

Return to your rest, my soul,
for the LORD has been good to you.

—PSALM 116:7

U narguably, one of the biggest differences between life in Uganda and life in the United States is the pace. Through a decade of living and raising children overseas, I've come to love the beautifully slow tempo of life and steady stream of unexpected visitors that comes with living in Uganda. Unpredictability is the only thing that is predictable. You can count on things not going according to plan, and you can count on abundant grace from your neighbors when they don't.

The contrast hit me hard when we first moved to the States. All I could think was, *Everything, everyone, is moving so fast.*

For the first few months, we hopped from one Airbnb to another in search of a rental house. It seemed we would never find something big enough for our family that was also within our relatively meager budget. Then one day some kind farmers from Iowa reached out to us. They had heard a bit of our story from a friend of a friend, and while they hadn't exactly been thinking of renting out the farm they'd recently bought, they'd be willing to if we wanted it. Every time I think of this, I marvel at how the Lord truly does provide for His people.

We drove over to check it out. I held my breath as we pulled up to the sprawling twelve acres complete with horses and two chicken coops in the back. Could this be it? The house was on a street called Retreat, and Benji and I both paused long when we read it on the street sign. *Retreat.* It was what we were desperately longing for, and we both felt that God had seen and heard our heart cries. *Retreat.* It felt like a lot more than a street name; it felt like a promise. A promise that, I admit, I did not grab hold of very quickly.

Instead, I occupied myself with all the tasks of resettling our family. I wanted desperately to find our community in this new place, to find jobs, find a church, connect with people. I wanted to help my children adjust to this new life with all its quirks and different ways of doing things. I stayed busy, busy, busy.

But six months in, as I described to my husband how frantic I had felt for the last season, how anxious to hold it all together, I realized that without knowing it and without wanting to, I had adapted to the frenzied pace that I disdained.

Really, the achiever in me already lives at this frantic pace on the inside, and living in a culture that affirms my desire to achieve and do and spin and run stirs up this tendency instead of mitigating it the way our often slow pace of life in Uganda did. As Benji and I talked it through, I realized that, to me, slow equaled unproductive and rest equaled weakness.

"Did you always have such high expectations of yourself?" someone once asked me. I laughed a little at the question. *High expectations? Me?*

The true answer, though, is yes.

In some ways, productivity is my love language. You need something? I can get it done. I perceive you need something? I'll probably do that too. No one is signing up to lead the event, committee, church play, women's conference? Sign me up. For years, any type of rest just felt . . . unproductive. And I don't think I'm alone in this.

How often do we answer the question of "How are you?" with "Good. Well, busy . . . but good. It's just been a busy week." And it has. It's just been a busy week/month/year/life. Or I also often hear "Exhausted. This week has been crazy." But it seems like the same people who were exhausted from a crazy week a few months ago are again exhausted this week.

Do you feel it too? And if our expectations of ourselves aren't already high enough, society heaps them on. We need to have a side hustle; we need to enroll our children in sports and clubs; we need to participate in all the church and school activities. We need to get our steps in; we need to have a tidy house and a manicured lawn; we need to have our nails and hair done. We must be busy; we must be successful; we must achieve and produce and go, go, go.

There isn't exactly anything wrong with being busy or having high expectations of ourselves or working hard. These can all be good things! Where it becomes dangerous is when we begin to define ourselves by what we can accomplish instead of through the lens of God's unearned, unmerited love. When doing takes priority over abiding in Him and dwelling with Him, we have made a dangerous turn. All this busyness can slowly reveal in me the incorrect thought that maybe by working hard enough, by producing enough, I will earn His love or favor. I know the truth that I am beloved without hustling or performing, without succeeding or achieving, but I have set my whole life up so that it doesn't actually *feel* like that is true.

Maybe because I tend to think the world depends on me. (Ugh. This is hard to admit.) Maybe because then I don't have to feel pain as deeply. If I pause long enough to rest, I have to feel, and sometimes the feeling is so painful that I just keep pushing through to avoid it. As I mentioned earlier, if I stay really busy, I don't have to ask myself the hard questions that come up in the quiet. *Am I really loved? Does anyone see me? Does my life matter at all?* Rather than fixing my eyes on Jesus as an alternative to my anxiety, I fill the space with tasks and

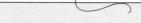

## RETHINKING OUR TO-DO LISTS

Practically speaking, how do we put these truths into practice? I'll share what has helped me over the past few months in thinking through my yeses, my nos, my God-given capacity.

I started simple. I grabbed a pen and paper and started writing down everything that was taking my time: responsibilities, kid stuff, work stuff, church stuff, home stuff, relationships. I even listed things that I wanted to get involved in if I could find time—a small group at church, volunteering once a week—and friendships I would like to pursue, rhythms I wanted to put in place. I held on to the list for a few days, asking myself why I would say yes to these things. Were they bringing me joy? Were they all necessary? Were there things I was doing out of guilt or obligation? Were there things I was saying yes to just so I wouldn't disappoint people?

I sat with my husband and children and we talked about our priorities. Time together each day is big for us, and this means saying no to a lot of after-school things so we can preserve a family meal around the table in the evening.

Could you make a similar list and ask yourself those questions? And then could you ask God which items He is calling you to say yes to in this season and which things you aren't meant to carry right now?

Just because you don't love it doesn't mean it has to go. On my list are things that bring me much joy, like homeschooling my

noise. The thing is, though, all the noise and busyness leave me feeling, once again, pulled apart. Anxious.

Can you relate? What is keeping you busy, pulling you from one

children and trying to complete this book. There are things that
don't bring me a ton of joy but are necessary for my family's func-
tioning, like driving kids to school and after-school activities and
grocery shopping. Then there are the really heavy things that I
wish weren't on the list but I know are mine to carry in this season: walking with a loved one through an excruciatingly difficult
illness, reaching out to someone who is very hard to love, going
to therapy weekly even on the days when I don't want to show
up and deal with my stuff.

There may be some things that you said yes to in the past that
you have to say no to in this current season, not because you
don't care or because these things aren't important but because
there are other things God is asking you to focus on right now.
There might be things you are saying no to today that you will be
able to say yes to in the future.

I invite you to make your list and to place everything on your
list before God, who knows your frame, your capacity, and your
limits. Ask Him to show you what stays and what goes, what
works and what doesn't. You might be surprised to find that His
expectations of you don't look a whole lot like the ones you have
put on yourself.

Say yes to your most important things so that you can walk in
the calling God has given you. Even the heaviest and hardest
things will ultimately bring about peace when you are walking in
obedience to Him.

place or thought to the next, occupying your mind so that you don't "have the time" to cry out to God with your grief or to notice the evidence of His goodness all around you and to worship? Have you absorbed the thinking that your value might come from what you do or accomplish or that to be faithful to God, you have to be "doing something for Him"?

We run frenzied from one place or appointment to another. Our minds spin with a million things that we believe we need to do. We are going, going, going, achieving, climbing the ladder of success . . . for what exactly? To fall into bed at the end of the day exhausted and do it all over again tomorrow? We *know* that there has to be more than this, that God created us for more than this, but try as we might, we just can't seem to get off the hamster wheel.

Whenever I stretch myself too thin, I start to feel frantic. I become wildly busy but rarely productive. I begin to feel that no matter what I am doing, I should be doing something else, and nothing that I am doing is ever enough. I jump from one thing to another, not doing any of it well. Recently, I knew it was getting out of control when one minute I was complaining to Benji that I didn't have enough time or margin to do everything that was required of me and the next minute I was volunteering to lead a women's conference at the church we had joined a month earlier.

So often, our anxiety is fueled by the very busyness that we thought might distract us from our worries in the first place! Perhaps we need to consider whether some of the things filling our calendar and our days should be let go, leaving space not only for time with Jesus but also for the deep rest our bodies and souls need.

Around the time we moved, I read an article on re-entry for missionaries that said we are addicted to being needed. It struck a deep chord. Losing my familiar place of ministry and service left me feeling lost, purposeless. I threw myself into being a mom—*I would be the best one ever!*—but that came up short too. I chided myself every time I couldn't be exactly what my children needed or take away their pain or make life easier for them. So then I threw myself into anything and everything that came my way, without ever stopping to think about why.

Who was I trying to prove myself to?

What was I trying to prove?

My worth? My value?

Is all my striving serving only to push me further into fear and anxiety?

Certainly, we *are* called by God to love our neighbor as ourselves. The desire to serve, help, and love is a beautiful reflection of the heart of Christ, and even as I have wrestled with saying yes too much and overestimating my capabilities, I still believe that Jesus wants His children to be servants of people. But Jesus also charges us to "be wise as serpents."[1] When our service and help isn't wise, when we aren't discerning about where we help and serve or where we say yes, we quickly come up empty. After all, we are human. God made us that way.

Remember how Psalm 103:14 says He shows compassion on His children because "he knows our frame; he remembers that we are dust" (ESV)? This gives me so much comfort! He knows my frame. He knows that I have human limits, capacity. All these expectations to do, do, do and go, go, go? God didn't put them on us; we put them on ourselves. And in doing so, we are pulling ourselves apart, away from wholeness, away from shalom.

So what might happen if we started acknowledging—and even embracing—our limits?

C∽

WHEN JOHN THE Baptist first shows up in John's Gospel, he announces his presence with a strange and profound statement.

There was a man sent from God, whose name was John. He came as a witness, to bear witness about the light, that all might believe through him. . . .

And this is the testimony of John, when the Jews sent priests and Levites from Jerusalem to ask him, "Who are you?" He confessed, and did not deny, but confessed, "I am not the Christ."[2]

The first thing John says about himself isn't who he is but rather who he *isn't*: "I am not the Christ." Here is John, sent from God, being questioned by the priests and the Levites, the religious leaders of the time. Surely, he needs to tell them of his importance and make

## RESTING SPACE

What is helping me make time to rest is to ask myself some questions:

- *Do I have to do it now?*
- *Is there something that can wait?*
- *Can I fill this space with Jesus somehow? Through a podcast, an audiobook or Bible app, worship music?*
- *Can I do what I need to do and still find time for His presence, still sit surrendered at His feet?*

As you intentionally pause to consider where you might make space to rest, remember that "sitting at Jesus's feet" doesn't always have to mean actual sitting. We can bring hearts of rest to Jesus as we pick up our groceries and drive to work. But we also need to carve out times or days to let some things slide so that we can be intentional in our worship and time with Him.

sure they understand that he has authority, that he has been sent by God Himself. He should probably recount for them the number of people he has baptized into repentance so that they will take him seriously. He should mention that God spoke of Jesus to John even while he was still in the womb.[3] That is pretty impressive stuff.

So what does he answer?

John replied in the words of the prophet Isaiah, "I am the voice of one crying out in the wilderness, 'Make straight the way of the Lord.'"[4] That's it. *I am a voice. I am pointing people to Him. I am preparing a way.*

John's entire purpose on earth is to point people to Jesus so that

---

Rest is not for weak people, for lazy people, for unproductive people. Rest is for obedient people. For hardworking, highly capable people like Martha and you and me.

I want to challenge you today to put something away, to let something slide. Don't skip a meeting and lose your job or leave your kids to walk home from school in the rain or something, but maybe read a few pages of a book instead of doing one final load of laundry. Maybe spend some time in the quiet after the kids go to bed instead of flipping on the TV. Maybe throw something easy in the microwave for dinner and play on the floor with your little one instead of preparing an elaborate meal. Or you can be a little crazy like me and get a few chickens, just so you can sit next to them for a while and watch them run around and do their silly dances and tip their heads up quirkily to swallow their water, just so you can remember God, who created all things so beautifully and perfectly and who cares for the sparrows and certainly won't forget about you.

they might be saved. His sole desire is to bring people to Christ. He lets all the rest of it fall to the side, not even worthy of mention. No accomplishments matter here. No titles, successes, or failures make a difference. John lives to have relationship with God and point people to Jesus, and the very first step here is to acknowledge *I am not the Messiah. I am here to make Jesus known.* I can love and I can serve, but I will never be all things to all people, and I wasn't meant to be. I am not the Christ.

The following day, John sees Jesus coming. "Behold, the Lamb of God!" John proclaims, "I have seen and have borne witness that this is the Son of God."[5] *Look!* he says. *Look at Jesus!* I want my life to be more like this. I want my conversations and interactions to be less about who I am or what I have done and more about who He is and what He has done for us. I want my life to testify of His goodness.

In order to do this, I am going to have to slow down. I am going to have to say no to some things so that I can say yes to the most important things, the things that God has given me to do, the people God has given me to love. When we learn to say wise nos so that we can give our best yes, we interrupt our anxiety spiral and inch closer to the peace God longs to give us.

So how do we know where to say yes and where to say no? In his letter to the Philippians, Paul prays that they would be able to discern what is best for the glory of God,[6] and I pray this for us too. We need to ask God to help us discern when our yeses are furthering His kingdom and bringing Him glory and when they are simply keeping us busy or keeping up appearances. In his letter to the Colossians, Paul says it like this: "We continually ask God to fill you with the knowledge of his will through all the wisdom and understanding that the Spirit gives, so that you may . . . please him in every way: bearing fruit in every good work, growing in the knowledge of God."[7]

If something that we are involved in isn't bearing fruit in our lives, isn't helping either us or someone we are in relationship with grow in the knowledge of God, it might not be the very best use of our time. If we are diving into something to prop up our own egos, prove that we can be all things to all people, or simply keep up with the demands of the world, it might be time to reevaluate. God will give us wisdom as we bring our to-do lists and commitments to Him.

I don't like to say no, and I'm guessing you feel the same. We are terrified of disappointing anyone. But what does this say about us? Once again, though it is difficult and embarrassing to type out, my aversion to disappointing others suggests that I think I can be the savior. My reluctance to say no reveals something deeper in my heart: a desire to be all things for all people. On the surface, this may sound kind, even generous, but dig a little deeper and it might reveal that slowly, without realizing it, I slip myself back into the place of God. I will fix it. I will help you. I will comfort you. I will provide for your needs.

Talk about burdensome! How can we have peace if we believe it all depends on us?

This is an ongoing battle for me, but I see progress. I believe my family does too and feels the deep peace that comes from having parents and a home that are not perfect but also not stretched too thin.

Too many yeses leave us exhausted and frantic, unable to give our best yes to the Lord and our people. What I am learning (slowly) is that sometimes we have to say no to what is good so that we can say yes to what is better.

JUST AS JESUS beckons His disciples to come away with Him to a quiet place to rest, just as He Himself slips away often to be with the

Father in the quiet, God offers us rest and retreat. But we have to be attentive to His call and active in receiving it.

Luke 10:38–42 tells us the story of sisters I love, Mary and Martha of Bethany. These two, along with their brother, Lazarus, who Jesus will later raise from the dead, are dear friends of Jesus's. I love imagining them opening their home to Jesus and the disciples anytime they came through town, the deep camaraderie that developed over bread and wine around their table.

Luke observes that, after welcoming Jesus and His disciples, Martha busies herself with the preparations of the meal as Mary sits at His feet listening to His teaching. Martha is so preoccupied with getting everything just right, so busy with everything that she believes needs to be done, that she is missing out on Jesus right in front of her. *Jesus is at her house!*

And I feel the tension. I would *want* to sit at the feet of Jesus if He came to my house, but I know that I would also feel a deep need to make sure everything was exactly perfect. Anyone who knows me well can imagine me in this moment, wiping the counters and compulsively rearranging the throw pillows on the couch for the hundredth time.

As Martha races around and eventually becomes annoyed with Mary's lack of help, Jesus consoles her. He says, "Martha, Martha, you are worried and upset about many things, but few things are needed—or indeed only one. Mary has chosen what is better, and it will not be taken away from her."[8]

Mary has chosen to rest at the feet of Jesus. She has left work undone for the better thing that is right in front of her. *Oh, that we would choose the better thing.*

I believe that one of the Enemy's most effective strategies to separate us and distract us from Jesus is to keep us really busy. We are doing good things. Things that have to be done. Things that are of

God, even. But are we enjoying God Himself, looking to God, communing with God, *resting* in God? Martha is doing important things. But she is missing the deep and abiding peace that would come from just sitting with Jesus, who calls her beloved.

In Exodus, when God first instructs His people to observe Sabbath, He says that it will be a sign between His people and Him that He is the Lord.[9] We don't just rest to recharge. We don't just rest because God commanded it. We rest as a way of saying to Him, "You are God, and I am not."

When we rest, we lay our idol of control and self-sufficiency at His feet. We say, *You are in charge here.* Rest is just another way we trust Him, another way we surrender.

I'll admit, even growing up as a believer, I never really understood Sabbath, at least not the way it had been explained to me. Was I really supposed to just leave the dirty dishes piled in the sink on Sunday? What does "doing no work" actually mean?

When we dig into Scripture, we see that observing Sabbath doesn't mean just abandoning our necessary tasks and responsibilities. In the Old Testament, the Israelites had very specific things that they still had to do on the Sabbath day, the day set apart to rest and worship God. They had to bring certain animals to sacrifice and sacrifice them in different ways. Sometimes they had to prepare food, and other times they were instructed to prepare the food beforehand. Regardless, Sabbath wasn't just "doing nothing"; it was a time to set aside ordinary work in order to worship God and bask in His goodness.

Sabbath means acknowledging that even if we do all the things, there will still be more to do. Our work will never end, and so *we must learn to trust God with the things left undone.* We can pause our insanely busy schedules to be with Him, to worship Him, to simply enjoy Him the way we would the company of a great friend. We can do it on Sunday, or we can do it in the middle of this day. We can pause and look into the eyes of a loving Father who can be trusted to take care of the things that don't get done today, who can be worshipped long before our tasks are all accomplished.

I don't like to think of the moments at Jesus's feet that I have missed over the past year because I was so deeply committed to getting everything done. I let the *good* get in the way of the *necessary*.

If you are like me and rest is a struggle, I know what you might be thinking: *But I have to clean the house. I have to drive the kids to the things. I have to work. I have to finish the laundry and make dinner and put everything back in order.* Yes, you do, eventually. God isn't asking us to abdicate all responsibility and veg out. But I do believe He is asking us to schedule in margin and time to sit at His feet, time to worship Him as a priority and not as an afterthought. Some of the things we have to do don't need to be done right now if our bodies or our minds need to rest, if we need to pause to be present, if we haven't yet made space to worship and adore Him today, or if our anxiety is again pulling us apart.

When we stop our work to enjoy God and His creation and His people, not just on Sunday but on any day, we say, *Lord, You are God of all of it. You are God of the things I left undone today and the things I simply cannot do.* As we take time to rest, to Sabbath, our illusion of control fades, our trust increases, and so does our peace.

IF WE'RE HONEST, of course, not all of our busyness is rooted in productivity. Many of us keep our minds occupied with less useful things like bingeing on Netflix, scrolling through Instagram, laughing at TikTok, or shopping online.

This could be a whole separate chapter, or probably even a book, but I am convinced that nothing is robbing us of peace more than the constant comparison and information overload coming from the little computers we carry around in our pockets all day. The human brain simply wasn't designed to sift through this much information.

There are seasons when I find myself able to use social media as an encouragement and a way to get information, seasons when I don't fall prey to quite so much comparison or anxiety as I read, but most of the time it is adding more anxiety and stress. When I return to Instagram after taking a break from it, I can feel the shift in my brain, the anxiety and depression rising as I scroll through other people's picture-perfect. By contrast, saying no to endless information via technology allows me to be present and gives space for mental and emotional rest.

Busyness of any kind, whether productive or not, can become an addiction, a way of numbing our minds to push back our anxieties. Like any addiction, busyness may keep us from feeling pain for a while. But it also isolates us from those we love and interferes with what really matters, stealing our peace and steadfastness.

I am learning that my nos, when well thought through and intentional, create time for better yeses—more Jesus, more grounding, more mundane serving my people with doing the dishes and making the dinner, more Lego towers and homework help. No is often the key to my very best yes.

When I intentionally put my busyness away and make time for real rest with my Father, I find what I knew to be true all along: I am dearly loved. I am seen by a God who adores me. I don't have to strive and I don't have to hide. He alone is in control. He alone is trustworthy to hold it all. I am invited to *retreat* here at His feet.

You know what is so beautiful? All our idols—control, anxiety, approval, comparison—demand *more* of us. They all compel us to try harder, move faster, achieve. But our God? He asks us for less. He asks us to rest. To lay aside climbing that ladder and working and striving so that we can sit at His feet like Mary, to remember who He is and worship Him for it. To trust Him.

Psalm 116:7 beckons, "Return to your rest, my soul, for the LORD has been good to you." When we learn to rest, we say that we trust Him. When we learn to rest, we say that we believe we are loved no matter what we achieve or accomplish. When we learn to rest, we say, not just with our lips but with our whole lives, "The Lord has been good."

During my fifteen years of living in Uganda, the only things I really missed about Tennessee were people and fall. After our return to the States, about midway through October I looked up. The leaves were red and gold, the air crisp, and the sunshine bright. Fall was my favorite season as a child, and in the year-round heat of the equator, I hadn't experienced an autumn in more than a decade. I realized as I looked around that fall—the season I had so looked forward to enjoying, surrounded by the changing leaves of the incredible trees all over our property—was almost over, the ground already covered with leaves and the branches quickly becoming bare. I had been so fixated on everything that needed to get done that I had hardly paused to lift my eyes and look around. How much beauty and provision had I missed out on because I was "so busy"? Was I turning my gaze away from my good God and the retreat and peace He wanted to give me because I thought I could get things done and keep the world spinning on my own?

I began to realize that no matter where I was in the world, margin was not going to just appear on my calendar. I would have to create it. My busyness was just another way that I wasn't trusting God.

Might this be true for you in your busyness as well? If so, I hope you'll join me in choosing to believe that the God who feeds the birds and clothes the lilies and causes the trees to light with flame *is* going to take care of us and our people. When we rest, when we resist the lure of the to-do list, we declare it boldly: Not only has the Lord been good, but *He will continue to be good.*

⁓

I TOOK MY kids to buy chickens at Tractor Supply yesterday. We came home with eight chirping babies to put in the warming box the little guys and I had prepared the night before. My teenagers rolled their eyes at me, and my husband just smiled knowingly.

Why did I buy these chickens? I am not totally sure. I don't need another project. I'm clearly still in the thick of it with transition and struggling to manage schedules and acclimate to the pace of life here. It's winter, so the chicks will have to live inside for at least the next six weeks.

But yesterday the sun peeked out for long enough to remind me that spring is coming, and I began craving signs of new life. New life in me and new life around me. Plus, my little Ugandan-born farm boy has been begging for chickens ever since we landed in this rental home with ready-made coops.

So instead of cleaning the house or doing the laundry or working on my endless to-do list, I spent the majority of the day sitting with my five- and three-year-olds in my lap, watching eight little chicks run around and peck and jump on top of each other and spill their food and water. *Look at the birds,* Jesus instructed, and we laughed at how these little birds at just one day old already knew exactly what to do to eat and drink and stay warm. I was wildly unproductive. And it was the most joy-filled and peaceful I have felt in a while.

On this gray Saturday morning, this was my soul's small way to exhale and say, *Lord, You are God of the things left undone today, and I am allowed—in fact, instructed—to enjoy You and Your creation.*

I guess what I am trying to say is there is time for chickens; we just have to make it. There is margin to enjoy the things God has created, even if they serve no other purpose but to bring us joy and remind us of His goodness. After all, it is in His goodness that we find our deep and abiding peace.

There is time and room and freedom to not express our opinions or comment about everything online, room to still be learning and growing in the here-and-now world. We are allowed to be unproductive, to leave our phones on silent in the other room and watch the chickens or dig our hands into the soil of a garden or read a book or just breathe.

There is time for joy. There is time for chickens. And there is time to sit at the feet of Jesus and *rest*.

*Father, we confess that we often long to be all things to all people, even though we know that You alone are all they need. Give us wisdom with our yeses and nos; give us discernment to know when it is time to work and when it is time to rest. Remind us that Your love for us is not tied to our productivity or our achievements. We choose rest as a way to worship. We choose rest as a way to trust You with what is up ahead and with what remains undone today. Help us choose the better thing: You. Amen.*

# 16

---

# THE MINISTRY
# OF RECONCILIATION

*Practice 8: Embracing Forgiveness*

In Christ God was reconciling the world to himself, not
counting their trespasses against them, and entrusting to
us the message of reconciliation.

—2 CORINTHIANS 5:19, esv

That same daughter that got caught in the rapids with me over
a year ago? She sat me down the other day. "Someone mentioned that you said this thing about me," she said, "and it
really hurt." I sank to the floor. "It's one thing to have the community
make comments, but when it's your own family, it really stings."

*Talk about wanting to run and hide in the bushes.* Here was one of
the people I adore most in the whole world, a person I would do
absolutely anything for, telling me that I had hurt her—and I had no
defense. I had actually done the things she was talking about. I was
embarrassed, ashamed, gutted.

"You are right," I said softly. "I did that. I hate that I did that. Will
you forgive me?"

"Of course," she said. Grateful for her grace undeserved, I was
still devastated by my sin.

*We've all been there.* The truth is, we can't walk in the peace of
God when we aren't in right relationship with the people around us.

And we can't walk in the peace of God if we are walking in habitual patterns of sin.

This sin was specifically against a person, and it is easy to see how I hurt her and how my sin affected our relationship. I ran my mouth when I should have kept it shut. But the effects of our sin always reverberate. Even sin that we think might affect only ourselves is hurting others and, worse, hurting our relationship with God.

Scripture is clear that all of us "fall short of the glory of God,"[1] and that means we are all going to hurt each other. All of us are going to disappoint each other more than we would like to admit. As much as I wish I would never wrong my people, it's usually those closest to us who witness our sin. And sin is ugly.

Distraction.

Discontent.

Selfishness.

Prejudice.

Addiction.

Pornography.

Dishonesty.

Comparison.

Idolatry.

Whatever form it takes, sin always robs us of our peace.

Israel is such a clear picture of this throughout all the Old Testament. When the people of Israel are in right relationship with God, they flourish. When the people turn to patterns of sin, the nation begins to crumble, enemies invade, and the people are captured or exiled. I'm not suggesting that if we obey God and repent of our sin, it will be smooth sailing from here on out and we will avoid suffering. We know this isn't true. But I am suggesting that we will not fully experience the peace of God if we are walking in unrepentant sin. Sin causes our lives to crumble.

Our kind and loving Father *longs* to pour out His favor and His peace on His people. In the Old Testament, God longs to provide for the Israelites' physical needs—beautiful land and lush fruit and large harvests—as well as their spiritual needs—peace and favor and *nearness to God*. He longs to walk among them and be in deep relationship with them. And He longs for this nearness with us too. He is a good God who desires to draw near to us and walk among us and who, through His Son, has made a way for this to be possible.

I certainly don't believe that *all* hardship and suffering is a direct result of disobedience, unforgiveness, or a lack of trust in God, and if you are going through something excruciating, please don't misunderstand me to say that this suffering is your fault. It could be a direct effect of disobedience, but it also *could not be,* and I can't decide that for you. We know that some suffering and hardship is just the result of living in this broken, fallen world. Remember Job?

If you are struggling with chemical imbalances, true depression, anxiety, or other mental illness, I don't believe that this is some kind of punishment for disobedience or the result of it. If you are in the deep, dark struggle of mental illness, oh, friend, I am so sorry. I see you and I love you and I have been there. God is near to you even as you fight this.

But I do believe that our "little" disobedience, our distractions and numbing, our unforgiveness or refusal to repent for the way we have wronged others, and our idols that turn our eyes from Jesus are increasing our anxiety, individually and as a society. I say that with exactly zero condemnation because I am so guilty of falling prey to this. I say it knowing how quickly my own anxiety spikes when I am mired in self-pity, when I turn my eyes and my heart from God and focus on other things, when I let how I feel dictate what I believe about Him instead of letting His Word remind me of who I am. And I say it picturing our good God, a deeply loving Father, who wants to dwell among His people and longs to give them peace and His presence if only they would turn their eyes away from their tasks and their prideful defense and their iPhones to seek His face.

In the Gospels, we see Jesus eating with and speaking to sinners, and when He was criticized, He told onlookers that He came to save not the healthy but the sick. *The sick*—those of us who do not do what we want to do and do what we don't want to do![2] Jesus paid for our sin because He wants to be *near* us. Let's go back to the parable of the prodigal son, who was clearly walking in disobedience and disrespect toward his father. My favorite children's Bible, *The Jesus Storybook Bible* (which I have used to teach tons of adult Bible studies, by the way), tells the story this way:

> All this time, what [the son] doesn't know is that, day after day, his dad has been standing on his porch, straining his eyes, looking into the distance, waiting for his son to come home. He just can't stop loving him. . . .
>
> The dad leaps off the porch, races down the hill, through the gap in the hedge, up the road. Before his son can even begin his I'm-Sorry-Speech, his dad runs to him, throws his arms around him, and can't stop kissing him.[3]

It's an adaptation of the biblical story, yes, but it presents such a beautiful—and accurate—picture of the character and heart of our Father. The illustration in the book shows the excited father leaping, racing toward his son. *Our God always comes for us, always after us, always calling us home.*

What a model of reconciliation! And because we know we are loved like this by our Father, we can repent of our sin like the prodigal son did. I hope that as you do this, you will be met with the immense grace that my daughter and other members of my family and close friends of mine so kindly pour out on me in forgiveness. But even if you aren't, even if the person you have wronged stares back in unforgiveness, you have a Father with His arms open wide to you.

We are reconciled because of Jesus. God provides a perfect sacrifice in Jesus so that we do not have to run *from* Him when we mess up but can instead run *to* Him.

IN LEVITICUS, GOD gives His people instructions and guidelines for life because He wants them to choose wisely. He wants them to choose peace and provision and relationship with Him.

> If you follow my decrees and are careful to obey my commands, I will send you rain in its season, and the ground will yield its crops and the trees their fruit. . . .
>
> I will grant peace in the land, and you will lie down and no one will make you afraid. . . .
>
> I will put my dwelling place among you, and I will not abhor you. I will walk among you and be your God, and you will be my people.[4]

But the Israelites are easily distracted, and so am I.

One thing God warns Israel about frequently is their idols. For the Israelites, these were usually statues of false gods, and it is easy to take a quick inventory of my own life and say confidently, "I don't have this problem. No fake god statues around here."

My idols aren't as easily seen and thus are easier to ignore, but it doesn't mean they aren't there. My desires for control, for approval, for success, for busyness and distraction that numb me to the pain around me, my pride and my unforgiveness of others—all of these can slip into idol territory so quickly. My reliance on my emotions rather than on the truth of God's Word or my trust in my own abilities rather than in God's sovereignty leads to idols in my life that need to be uprooted for me to live in the peace of Christ.

Remember Gideon? Once Gideon had doubted, questioned, offered thanks, and then named the place "The LORD Is Peace," God led him to destroy the idols of His people.[5] He has to tear down his own idols and the idols of his people in order to truly worship God.

When we turn away from our idols of control, busyness, feelings,

## MAKING THINGS RIGHT

This isn't the most fun exercise, so be gentle with yourself. Ask the Lord to call to mind your sin. "Search me, O God, and know my heart," David cries out in the Psalms. "See if there is any wicked way in me."[11] This can be a scary thing to ask. But God *will* reveal your sin, and He will do it gently because He is kind.

As He brings things to mind, stop and repent. Right now, tell Him how sorry you are for the ways you have sinned against Him. If this sin necessitates a change in habit, write it down. If this sin requires an apology to another person you have wronged, make the phone call. Set up the coffee date. Do not apologize in a text message.

Practice looking the people you have hurt in the eye and saying, "I am sorry. I sinned against you. Will you please forgive me?"

The flip side of this is asking God if you are holding unforgiveness in your heart toward someone else. This is sin too. If that person has already apologized, it might be time to let it go. Ask the Lord to give you a heart of forgiveness. Often when I am holding unforgiveness in my heart toward someone, I ask God to distraction, pride, (fill in the blank with yours here), we make space for God to pour out His peace and favor. When we turn our eyes from the other glittery things that are distracting us, the other goals that we are fixated on, we make space to *see* God's favor, presence, peace, and goodness poured out on our lives. We can be thankful for what we have instead of comparing and coveting. We can lament our losses and trust Him with them instead of wallowing in self-pity, bit-

---

call to mind my own sin, all the ways I have hurt Him and others, and how that sin put Him on the cross. Sometimes remembering how deeply and thoroughly I have been forgiven even when I didn't deserve it makes forgiving someone who has wronged me a little easier.

If the person you are holding unforgiveness toward hasn't apologized, there are probably a few options:

Maybe they don't know that they have hurt you. We are often quick to hold a grudge but slow to tell the truth when someone has wronged us. Don't assume they know and wait for an apology. Make the phone call or sit down with that person (once again, no text messages here) and tell them how you are hurt. You might be surprised at how quickly they apologize.

Or maybe the person you are holding unforgiveness toward isn't going to apologize or they apologize with their words but don't change their behavior. This is hard. In Christ, we are still called to forgive. You may not be able to walk in close relationship with someone who is unwilling to do the work on their end to reconcile, but you can ask the Lord to give you forgiveness in your heart toward this person. You can let go of bitterness and walk in forgiveness and peace, even with boundaries.

terness, or unforgiveness. We can rejoice in our gifts and the Giver instead of focusing on our lack. We can rest in His presence instead of endlessly striving. And when we realize our own sin and depravity, we make space for reconciliation—with God, and with others.

We shy away from this question because it is uncomfortable, but is there sin in your life that needs to be confronted? What are you most tempted to love more than God? What are you putting your trust in aside from Him? Where are you finding your identity, your affirmation, your joy?

*We become like what we worship.* I want to be more like the Prince of Peace. And I want to then carry His good news to others.

In his second letter to the Corinthian church, Paul urges them to remain true to their faith and turn from their sin.

> [God] through Christ reconciled us to himself and gave us the ministry of reconciliation; that is, in Christ God was reconciling the world to himself, not counting their trespasses against them, and entrusting to us the message of reconciliation. Therefore, we are ambassadors for Christ, God making his appeal through us. We implore you on behalf of Christ, be reconciled to God. For our sake he made him to be sin who knew no sin, so that in him we might become the righteousness of God.[6]

Paul loves the Corinthian church. Adores them. But the Corinthian church is a disaster. Their list of sins makes mine look not that bad. (I'm joking.) And in the middle of two long letters calling them out for their sin and urging them to walk in new ways, Paul shares the very Gospel of peace in four verses.

First, God through Jesus makes a *completely undeserved* way for us to be reconciled to Himself. Because of the first sin in the garden, because of the sin we see so clearly in our everyday lives, it should be impossible for us to be in relationship with Holy God. *But Jesus makes a way.* He takes the punishment our sin deserves and offers grace and forgiveness instead.

*And then He invites us to call others into this beautiful forgiveness.* We have a part to play. Paul calls us messengers of reconciliation, saying that God has entrusted to us the amazing task of telling other people about Him, and not just with our words but with our very lives!

We can't do this unless we are in right relationship with Him and then in right relationship with others. Nobody wants to hear the message of reconciliation from someone who isn't walking in right relationship with their family, their friends, and even their enemies. Just like the Corinthians, we need to tear down our idols, uproot the sin in our lives, and look to Jesus as the only one worthy of our worship and adoration so we can call others to Him.

I KNOW I am unusually blessed that my daughter came straight to me with the truth of how I wounded her, as I described at the start of this chapter, and that she was able to respond to me in forgiveness and grace. I didn't deserve this. And while this is exactly how a situation like this *should* go, especially as believers, it so often isn't this easy.

We let hurts fester and we shy away from addressing them, from telling someone the truth of how they have hurt us. Instead, we pretend that we are okay and decide we just won't share with that person, trust that person, or invite that person anymore. We stop responding to texts or we don't try very hard to make time to hang out. We ghost. We cancel. We pretend we have forgiven without ever giving the other person an opportunity to apologize. We stay divided, pulled apart, pulled away from relationship. Our internal anxiety increases.

But here is what I know: When we trust in the sovereignty of God, when we believe that He is using all things for good and for His purposes, we can speak the truth of our situation, we can humbly confess and apologize when we have gotten something wrong, and we can lavish grace and forgiveness on those who have wronged us.

Sadly, we are quick to justify our sinful behavior and then quick to justify our unforgiveness. *But she hurt me. No one will ever understand what that person did to me.* But when we think of what our sin did to Jesus, the undeserved punishment and torture He faced, no sin against us can compare. In Philippians 2, Paul urges his friends to have the same mindset as Christ Jesus,

> who, being in very nature God,
>> did not consider equality with God something to be used to
>> his own advantage;
> rather, he made himself nothing
>> by taking the very nature of a servant,
>> being made in human likeness.
> And being found in appearance as a man,
>> he humbled himself
>> by becoming obedient to death—
>>> even death on a cross![7]

Jesus loved us to death.

Could we even possibly love like this? Could we even possibly have this same attitude?

You might be thinking, *Well, Jesus was sinless, so He could do that, but I can't.* (We are so good at excusing ourselves.) Let me remind you that we have beautiful examples throughout all of Scripture of this lavish forgiveness both before and after Jesus. Remember Esau? Jacob had lied about him, stolen from him, and run away from him. Esau was so angry and hurt that he wanted to kill his brother. But when Jacob returns to Esau twenty years later, limping, trembling, Esau embraces him in love and forgiveness.

And as we saw in chapter 5, Jacob says that seeing Esau's face, receiving this kind of lavish forgiveness, "is like seeing the face of God."[8] This is what it is to be people of God. This is the ministry of reconciliation. When we can look into the face of someone who has deeply wounded us and we can see the face of God in them. When we can offer them the forgiveness that we ourselves have received from Christ. When we can look into the face of someone we have deeply wounded and can see the face of God in them and receive the forgiveness of God through them. Wholeness, shalom, in our relationships brings about wholeness in our hearts.

Later, we have Jacob's son Joseph looking into the faces of brothers who sold him, lied about him, and desired him dead. Joseph has suffered immensely as a result of their cruelty, and now he is in a position where he could let them starve. Yet when they come to him, trembling, fully aware that they should be paid back for all their sin, Joseph speaks these famous words: "You meant evil against me, but God meant it for good, to bring it about that many people should be kept alive, as they are today. So do not fear; I will provide for you and your little ones."[9] This is deep trust in a sovereign God. This is what it looks like to lay aside any idol of jealousy, comparison, bitterness, or anger and believe that God has a good plan and we can rest in it.

In Acts 7, in the midst of being stoned to death, Stephen looks up to heaven and sees Jesus standing at the right hand of God. Just as with Jacob, seeing the face of God gives Stephen what he needs to live in His peace. As he is being hurt, stoned, murdered, Stephen calls out, "Lord, do not hold this sin against them." He forgives, and he asks God to forgive. And do you know who was standing in the crowd watching, supporting the murder of Stephen? *Paul.* Paul, who would later call people all over the world to forgiveness, to the ministry of reconciliation.

Through each of these examples and more, we see that when we think of Christ and He fills our hearts with His peace, we can humble ourselves and admit the way we have sinned against God and others. We see that we can freely offer forgiveness no matter how hurt we have been. We can be reconciled to God and to others as we turn from our sin and walk in new ways. We can offer forgiveness and draw others into reconciliation because our peace comes from God and not perfect people or relationships. (These don't exist, by the way.)

Pride will keep us from this every time. Pride will keep us from admitting our sin and from forgiving others. But the humility of Christ will lead us to repent of our own sin, turn away from habitual sin and idols and distractions, and lavish grace on those who sin against us.

Please don't misunderstand. I'm not suggesting you put yourself at risk by staying in an abusive or toxic relationship. There are times when someone refuses to either repent of their sin or offer us forgiveness as we confess ours. Scripture is clear that we have to do everything we can, "as far as it depends on [us],"[10] to reconcile, but if the other person won't walk in it with us, we have to practice surrender again, trust God, and let that relationship go.

Others will hurt us; we will hurt others. Trying to defend ourselves will drain every last ounce of our peace. We aren't the judges. We can entrust ourselves and others to the God who judges justly (and so mercifully).

When we fully trust our good and kind Father, we can fully forgive. And as He alone equips us, we can walk as people of peace as we move into the world with His forgiveness and reconciliation.

*Father, we have sinned against You, yet You have removed our sin from us as far as the east is from the west in the sacrifice of Your Son, Jesus. We are so grateful. Search us and know us and see if there is any wicked way in us! We repent of the ways we have sinned against You and others, and we ask that You would bring our sin to mind quickly and then help us repent and walk in a new way. Father, help us forgive others freely just as You have forgiven us. We can't do it on our own, God. Fill us with Your love for the people around us. We love You. Amen.*

# 17

## A TOWEL AND A BASIN

### *Practice 9: Service*

Serve one another humbly in love.

—GALATIANS 5:13

After visiting roughly a million churches following our move to Tennessee, we finally settled on one we liked. Actually, I'm not sure if we even knew that we liked it or if we were just tired of looking. It was quite a bit less flashy than many we had visited, and the pastor raced to the back of the sanctuary to say hey at the end of the service because he noticed we were new. That was enough for us to come back for a second week in a row, something that we had not chosen to do at the other places we had visited. It helped that on our second visit, the announcements video glitched and someone had to stand up from the back and yell out the announcements. That felt like our kind of vibe.

The point is, once we decided that we were in, well, we were *all* in. We decided to make these people *our people,* and they decided to make us their people right back. They jumped in and served us wholeheartedly. They invited us over for meals and came to our house for meals. They came to our kids' basketball games and track meets. They showed up to help our teenagers get ready for prom.

The thing that was most impactful for me wasn't the food they brought or the rides they offered or the furniture they gave us, though that was all very much appreciated; the very best gift they gave was serving us with their time and their presence. Nothing filled me with joy and gratitude like when they would come over and just be with us. Lonely and missing my Ugandan home that was always full of people, I found that having someone come sit on my couch or around my table was the greatest gift.

When we felt alone, anxious, and unsettled, these people brought tangible peace into our home and our lives. As I think about them now, my eyes fill with tears of gratitude and I feel inspired to be more like this for others. Have you ever been loved like this? Does the thought of this kind of others-centered community spark something in you as well?

As you discern your yeses and your nos, as you set aside time to rest in God, and as you repent of sin and receive His deep forgiveness, might it be that He is urging you to plant a garden too? Not one with tomatoes and basil and watermelon, though if that's your thing, I hope you'll do that as well. But I think that a significant aspect of peace involves digging in deep with our communities, loving and serving the people right in front of us, and I fear that we are unable to do so because we have made ourselves far too busy with other, less vital things.

The ministry of reconciliation that Paul urges the Corinthians toward calls us not only to be in right relationship with God and others but also to be *messengers* of God's Gospel. And we cannot do this with just our words; we have to live it out in service to those around us. As we intentionally place our confidence in the One who is unshakable, we can begin to offer unshakable peace to the hurting and fearful people we encounter each day, living as vessels of God's peace in our chaotic times.

"BECAUSE WE LOVED you so much, we were delighted to share with you not only the gospel of God but our lives as well."[1] This verse—written by Paul, Silas, and Timothy regarding their time with the Thessalonians—hung on the wall for years in my home in Uganda as a reminder of how we wanted to live, how we actually did get to live: inviting people into our home, into our lives, serving and being served by our beloved community, sharing the Gospel not just in words but in a plate of rice and beans, a glass of water, a late-night hospital trip, a prayer in times of crisis, tears over hurting loved ones, laughter that made our bellies ache.

In his letter to the Galatians, Paul puts it this way: "You, my brothers and sisters, were called to be free. But do not use your freedom to indulge the flesh; rather, serve one another humbly in love."[2] Paul knows we are quick to imagine that freedom means we can do whatever we want. We *think* we want freedom to make our own choices, or freedom to be honored and highly esteemed, freedom to seek out the short-lived "peace" the world offers with a bubble bath and a glass of wine. But the freedom that Jesus gives us and calls us to is different. He frees us from our bondage, from our idols, from putting our confidence in our own fickle flesh that fails and disappoints time and time again. And, Paul says, He frees us to love our neighbor as we love ourselves. He frees us to serve. He frees us to follow *His* example.

Remember how Paul urges us in Philippians 2 to have the same attitude as that of Christ Jesus? The New King James Version of the Bible translates the chapter a little differently than how I have it memorized. Verse 7 reads that Christ "made Himself of no reputation." The footnote on this says that Christ "emptied Himself of His privileges." Can you imagine? We live in a world where we hold so tightly to our privileges, where our reputation is *everything* to us, but we are called to the humility of our King, who made Himself of no reputation, who emptied Himself of all privilege to serve us, to die for us.

In John 13, we see a beautiful illustration of this. The night before His death, Jesus has His disciples gathered together. He knows that one of the men at the table is about to betray Him and that He will then be tortured and die.

> He got up from the meal, took off his outer clothing, and wrapped a towel around his waist. After that, he poured water into a basin and began to wash his disciples' feet, drying them with the towel that was wrapped around him. . . .
>
> When he had finished washing their feet, he put on his clothes and returned to his place. "Do you understand what I have done for you?" he asked them. "You call me 'Teacher' and 'Lord,' and rightly so, for that is what I am. Now that I, your Lord and Teacher, have washed your feet, you also should wash one another's feet. I have set you an example that you should do as I have done for you."[3]

Jesus sets an example in His humility and then invites us to follow Him, to do the same. I don't know if you noticed this, but *Jesus washed Judas's feet.* Even after He knew that Judas would betray Him. Jesus loved and served even those He knew wouldn't love Him back. And He will give us the grace and the strength we need to serve, not for our own honor, not because we might be loved or served in return, but because in Him we have the freedom to love with abandon. The more we practice this, the more we believe it.

In a day and age when we think our image, our reputation, and our social-media following are our most powerful tools of influence, Jesus is beckoning us to a towel and a basin of water. Jesus is beckoning us to the freedom and peace of service.

WHEN WE FIRST found ourselves in the Nashville area, we spent at least one night a week working at the rescue mission. All our family members agreed that it was our favorite night of the week. We didn't know how long we would be here, we didn't yet have a stable housing situation, but it didn't matter. I knew deep in my heart and from lots of experience that serving together was an important part of our family culture and we would all begin to wither if we didn't find a place to plug in.

For those few hours of the week, our problems and our loneliness and our grief over all we had left behind faded away as we focused on loving someone else, even people we didn't know. For a few hours, we were filled with purpose as we mixed big vats of fruit salad and peeled potatoes and listened to stories of joblessness and homelessness and addiction and hardship and perseverance and renewed hope. We served up supper and warm smiles and extra-large glasses of chocolate milk. And our hearts filled with joy as we looked to meet the needs of others.

When we choose to serve, with our actions, with our time, with our listening, we say that another person's comfort is more important than our own. Another person's needs are more important than our own. Our own hardships suddenly don't seem quite so enormous.

A lifestyle of humility built on serving as Jesus did is another way that we choose to trust God. When we are serving because we are so full of the love of Jesus that we can't imagine *not* letting that flow out

## VESSELS OF PEACE

Do those around you see God's love, joy, and peace flowing through you into their lives? If not, what might be getting in the way?

What does—or what could—service look like in your life right now? Maybe it involves routinely volunteering or serving with your church or a charity, or maybe it means simply honoring the people in your life with your time, your listening ear, and your encouragement.

What work has the Lord appointed you to do in this season? Maybe it is something big, such as raising your children, loving your spouse, running a business, caring for a loved one. Or maybe it is something "small" (nothing done in obedience to the Lord is really small), such as remembering to lower your voice when you are frustrated instead of raising it, or making dinner (again!), or finishing a report.

Regardless of what He has called you to in this season, spend some time thinking about how you could do this with the same attitude as Christ: humbly, looking not to your own interests but to the interests of others.

Ask Him for help. We can't love like Jesus without His help.

Eyes up, love. Let's do this work undistracted and in compete obedience to Him. Here we will experience His deep peace that passes understanding.

of us, when we are truly putting the needs of others before our own out of genuine love and care, we can serve from a place of rest. As we enter into the pain of others, our pain grows less overwhelming because we are not alone in it. As we prioritize others—whether our families, our church small groups, or a stranger—by living in the humility and service God called us to, our worry for ourselves fades. Choosing others above ourselves, as backward and counterintuitive as it might seem, fills us with joy and deep satisfaction.

Generosity—with our time, with our things, with our homes, in our actions, in our service—shows our deep trust in God. As we share what we have, we say that we trust Him to provide all that we need. As we give of our time, we say that we trust Him with the things we may have to leave undone in order to listen well, love well, and invest our time in others. As we give of ourselves to our neighbor, we say that we trust Him to be our strength and to equip us for this service.

As we pour out His love to those around us, not only does our dependence on God increase our trust and peace but also we get to experience the deep joy of seeing and celebrating what He is doing in the lives of others, how He is providing for their needs, how He is answering their prayers. More reasons to trust. More reasons for peace.

I once heard Dr. Bryan Loritts observe that the place of our greatest service will become the place of our deepest satisfaction. This rang so true for me. God is incredibly kind to design us this way. As we pour out the joy, the love, the very peace that He has given us, these things don't decrease but multiply. I am not suggesting that service is some magical fix, but when we are actively loving and serving others, we can't simultaneously be as anxious about our own situations and our own needs.

Service and humility in themselves are acts of obedience to God. If the most important commands in all of Scripture are to love the

Lord with all our hearts, minds, and souls and to love our neighbor as ourselves,[4] we'd better believe that we cannot have peace when we are not doing these things.

In my own life, I have often experienced that there is no better way to know peace than practicing the humility of honoring others above myself. As I serve others, the anxiety and obsession about what is best for *me* falls away as I shift my thoughts and my focus to what is best for others. I experience a joy that I never could have known had I stayed wallowing in self-pity.

God wants our obedience because He knows that when we are living in the way He instructed us to live, our lives will be full of the good things He desires to give us. Loving and serving our neighbor will, without a doubt, lead to deeper peace, because it is the way God designed us to live. We need each other. This doesn't mean that our lives will be free from trouble and hardship, but as we shoulder each other's burdens, they become lighter. As we enter into the service of another, our joy and fulfillment, and therefore our peace and wholeness, increase.

I CAN IMAGINE you're thinking that *adding* something to your already full life doesn't seem like it could possibly bring peace. I know, just a couple chapters ago, I urged you to examine your yeses and nos with discernment and take some things off your calendar. So what is the difference between busyness that leads to anxiety and service that leads to peace?

I don't think Jesus is necessarily asking us to add another task or event to the calendar; instead, He is inviting us to a lifestyle that seeks the good of others above ourselves, that values the comfort and well-being of others enough to step in and love even when that requires sacrifice. There might be seasons of life when it looks like a weekly event on the calendar, but more often it can mean taking the extra five minutes to have a conversation with the grocery checkout person even when you are in a hurry or setting aside a task to be present with a child who needs your undivided attention. It can mean walking your leftover dinner across the street to an elderly neighbor or sending the text, making the phone call, or showing up with a coffee when a friend is hurting.

When we think about service, we can be prone to think about leaving everything behind to go on a shiny new adventure in a beautiful new place. I did that once. And it is true that the place of my greatest sacrifice became the place of my deepest satisfaction. Maybe God is calling you to that or will someday. We can tend to think of service as a once-a-week or once-a-month event, such as serving in a homeless shelter or soup kitchen like we did when my family first moved here. And God might be calling you to that too, especially in seasons when you have the margin and capability to do so. But service can be so much simpler than that. Service is a heart of hospitality, not just with our homes but with our *lives*.

Faithful obedience doesn't have to mean moving somewhere or doing some "big" or "important" ministry. Our small yes to God matters. And for you and me, today, it probably isn't anything flashy. It's probably wiping boogers or helping solve an algebra problem or smiling kindly at a stranger.

Faithful obedience can be opening our hands in surrender, again. Repenting of our sin, again. Walking humbly in a world that screams at us that reputation is everything. Emptying ourselves of privilege instead of grasping for it. Loving God and loving people in a million small ways.

Tearing down our destructive idols and practicing Helen Keller's self-forgetfulness lead to joy and peace. As we turn our eyes toward God, we can reach out our hands to love and serve others.

Imagine what would happen if we each took seriously Paul's challenge to the Philippians: "Do nothing out of selfish ambition or vain conceit. Rather, in humility value others above yourselves, not looking to your own interests but each of you to the interests of the others."[5] That sounds to me like a little taste of heaven on earth. If you and I want to experience this kind of community, we need to be willing to be the first to serve others. Be the friend you want to have. Be the community member you want to live near. Don't be afraid to be the first to serve, and watch as your community blossoms before you, creating security and peace that you never dreamed!

I REMEMBER HELPING with a friend's home birth. I cheered my friend on and encouraged her to breathe deep. As is typical in our little Ugandan town, the power was off. My friend had been laboring for almost twenty-four hours. She was tired; her husband was tired; the midwives were tired.

As everyone focused on helping mom through transition, a light caught the corner of my eye. Another friend and her daughter had crept downstairs from their apartment on the next floor. Silently, they laid trays of food on the counter before tiptoeing back upstairs. They had brought us dinner. Hours later, as the rest of us crooned over new life in the next room, these same friends came back and cleaned up, wiping up spills and removing all evidence of birth from the little apartment. I turned and watched them, their basins and towels, their quiet service, so beautiful.

When I think of people of peace, I imagine these friends, so full of the love and peace of God that they can humbly serve those around them. Not for accolades or praise but *for joy*.

I want this kind of humility, this kind of steadfastness. I want to be a person so filled with His peace that it overflows to my community in love and service to others. What if part of the deep peace we are missing is to be found in picking up a towel and a basin instead of wishing for a robe and a wine glass? Not only will we be more like Jesus when we make ourselves of no reputation, but we will *know more of Jesus* as we receive His invitation to love and serve our neighbors.

*Jesus, sometimes it is hard to fathom the mercy and kindness of Your sacrifice for us. How we long to live as examples of Your love and humility! We need Your help. Lord, strip us of our desire for accolades and praise, and give us hearts willing to be emptied of all privilege as we serve those around us. Cause us to be attentive to the needs of others, to be ambassadors of Your peace in our hurting world. Amen.*

# 18

## AN ETERNAL GLORY

*Practice 10: Waiting in Hope*

Our light and momentary troubles are achieving for
us an eternal glory that far outweighs them all.

—2 CORINTHIANS 4:17

"So, what are you guys looking forward to right now?" a friend asked the girls and me as we piled together on the couch a while back. Her innocent question was met with silence as we all looked uncertainly at one another.

Blank stares.

Crickets.

After multiple moves in our search for semi-permanent housing, on the heels of the shutdown-reopen-shutdown cycle of the global pandemic and multiple family emergencies, in a new place where we rarely ever knew what to expect, we had kind of just stopped getting excited. I wondered if we had forgotten how to look forward to anything, with so many expectations going unmet and so much being changed or canceled.

After all, if you don't hope for anything, you can't be disappointed.

As we contemplated our friend's well-intended question, I looked at my teenagers and saw that their faces reflected the weariness in my own heart. We didn't know how to make plans anymore without expecting that something would probably interfere with them. Looking forward to anything felt like setting ourselves up for disappointment. *Hoping felt like it might be a waste of time.*

I think of so many individuals whose plans and dreams have been shattered in these last years. Weddings were canceled. People were unable to travel to say goodbye to loved ones, unable to be with others during times of most importance. Jobs were lost, and school was closed, and any semblance of normal we thought we had flew out the window. Personally, and collectively, we have been shaken. Pain, grief, and fear all have a way of sucking the air out of the room, squeezing the delight and anticipation right out of us. Sometimes, getting excited about something that might happen in the future seems unwise, if not impossible.

But then I think of all the biblical characters who waited the better part of their lives—forty years, ninety years—for God to fulfill His promises. Some of them didn't even see the promises they were holding on to come to pass. There is Noah, climbing into the ark and waiting (appearing like a fool in the eyes of those around him) for water to fall from the sky. Waiting there in the dark as the waves crash against the side of a vessel he has built with his hands. Somehow waiting and believing that he and his loved ones will be safe and this storm will end, even when there is no sign of it. *Waiting in hope because he trusted in God.*

There is Abraham, finally receiving his promised son at one hundred years old.[1]

There is Moses, leading his people faithfully through the wilderness for forty years, rejoicing in God and testifying to who He is even after God has revealed to him that he will not enter the Promised Land himself. Many people like to say that the journey took so long because the Israelites were lost, but they weren't lost. God stayed with them the entire time. He led them in a pillar of fire and a pillar of cloud. The waiting was *intentional* on God's part. In the waiting, God grew Moses. God spoke to Moses. God showed Moses His glory.

I think of Joseph—hated by his brothers, sold into slavery as a "good alternative" to being murdered. How easy it would have been for him to despair! Joseph has heard from the Lord in two different dreams that seem to suggest that his family will one day bow to him,[2] but I would be willing to bet that it is pretty hard to hold on to that promise as he is chained and led away by slave traders to a foreign land. And although Joseph may not have known it at the time, as readers we know that it only gets worse. He will be falsely accused and even imprisoned long before what the Lord has spoken to him comes to pass. But he waited in hope because he trusted in God.

Only God in His providence could use all the *terrible* circumstances Joseph passes through to bring about His *good* purposes and plans. This is who God always is. This is what God does. Through Joseph's suffering, through Joseph's waiting, God will bring rich blessing to him and eventually save his whole family (and thus the lineage of Jesus). God is active and working, even in our hardship and distress, even in our waiting, even when the plan doesn't *look* good. Even when we can't see what He is doing, when we can't begin to imagine what we are looking forward to.

As I think of Joseph, as I think of these other biblical characters who waited long for the promises of God to come to pass, I understand that my own temptation in similar circumstances would be to complain to God, even to question Him. *Lord, how could You allow this to happen?* Or even, *Okay, God. I've been faithful and devout. I have done my best to flee temptation, and as if being a slave wasn't enough, now I am in prison?* I recognize the foolishness even as I type it, but I know my own heart enough to admit that these thoughts might sneak in. *I learned how to persevere in trial already, God. Can we be done with trial now?*

But Joseph isn't so foolish. His trust in the Lord and his devotion to Him doesn't waver in slavery, doesn't waver in temptation, and won't waver now, even in prison. The text reads, "The LORD was with Joseph,"[3] who was a slave in Potiphar's house, and everyone could see that the Lord was with him. The Lord is with Joseph in the midst of false accusations from Potiphar's wife for which, though he is thrown in prison, he could have easily been put to death. The Lord is with Joseph even in prison.[4] The Lord is with Joseph everywhere he goes, in every hardship, showing him mercy and granting him favor.

It's clear that the secret to Joseph's perseverance in trial is *God with him.* And in Christ, the same is true for us! No matter what depth of hardship we find ourselves in, *the Lord is with us* and wants to show us mercy and give us favor. We, too, can wait in hope because we trust in God. Can we have eyes open to see Him at work?

Paul puts it this way:

Therefore we do not lose heart. Though outwardly we are wasting away, yet inwardly we are being renewed day by day. For our light and momentary troubles are achieving for us an eternal glory that far outweighs them all. So we fix our eyes not on what is seen, but on what is unseen, since what is seen is temporary, but what is unseen is eternal.[5]

I think this is what Noah and Moses and Joseph all knew, that all the things we are waiting on here pale in comparison to what we are truly waiting on: eternity with God. We will walk again with Him in Eden forever, in perfect unity and peace. *This is the hope that can never disappoint.*

While Joseph is in prison for a crime he didn't commit, two of his fellow prisoners have dreams. Joseph pipes up that he can interpret them or, rather, that God will interpret them and show him what the dreams mean.[6] Joseph's total confidence in hearing from the Lord to interpret the dreams of the cupbearer and the baker indicate one thing for sure: Through years of waiting, terrible trials and hardships, persecution and false accusation, Joseph has remained in communication with his Father. He knows exactly where interpretations come from—God—and he is certain that He will give him the interpretations.

His hardship and waiting have not diminished his trust in God but increased it. We see evidence of this again, after Pharaoh puts him in charge of the entire country, and after his father and brothers join him in Egypt so they can live safely through famine. In what is maybe my favorite part of the whole story, Joseph, just before he dies, in the boldest, bravest, most certain hope, instructs his brothers to take his bones and his father's bones with them when they leave Egypt. Not *if* they leave Egypt, but *when*. "God will visit you and bring you up out of this land," Joseph tells his brothers.[7]

How does he know? *Because God promised.*

Nothing in Joseph's whole life has gone as planned. There has been disappointment after disappointment. Yet he believes with certainty that God is going to bring his family out of Egypt—even when it seems impossible—because God said so. How does he know? Because he knows who God is, a God who is always good and always using all for good, a God who always keeps His promises. How does he know? Because He has been faithful before. God has kept promises before. God has used the darkness for good before. Joseph's eyes are fixed not on what he can see but on what he cannot see: Eternal God.

Eternal glory with our kind and loving Father has been promised to us. We can stake our very lives on it. When nothing goes as planned, when we are faced with disappointment after disappointment, when there is nothing here in front of us to look forward to or hope for, we can shift our gazes to a certain God who makes certain promises, and we can trust that whatever we experience on earth will pale in comparison to the day we see Him face-to-face and then walk with Him *forever.*

It's startling to me how opposite I often am of these biblical heroes. I pray, and if I don't see results in the next few days, I despair. I whine. I let God know that *this is not fair.*

*How quickly I doubt the promises of God!* I know, beloved, so often our troubles don't feel "light and momentary"; they feel weighty and terribly difficult and all-consuming. But we have our certain hope in Jesus, who is coming back, who will wipe every tear from every eye, who will swallow up death forever.[8] I desire instead to eagerly anticipate the return of Christ, that perfect Revelation garden where we will live with Him forever. The certain promise that we can always, always look forward to.

One of my favorite parts of Exodus is chapter 15, commonly referred to as Miriam's song. The Israelites have come through the Red Sea on dry ground. They rejoice! God has made a way for them, and Miriam and the women of Israel dance and sing, waving their tambourines and timbrels. As I read that passage again recently, I realized they didn't find these tambourines in the desert; they brought their instruments with them. They looked at an impossible journey, at an uncrossable sea, and believed there would be rejoicing.

Miriam expected joy, anticipated that she would again worship God, even as she looked at the impossibility of the desert road. She grabbed her tambourine when there was nothing to sing about yet. She chose to anticipate joy, to believe in the promise and the presence of God.

*I want to live like this.*

We must shift our hope. We shift our hope from anything that we are looking forward to here on earth to the promises we have in Him. We shift our focus from our own agony, no matter how deep, to Jesus. Faith in God looks to the past to be reminded of our hope for the future. *Faithful He has been, faithful He will be, and ultimately, no matter what comes in this life, He will be victorious.* Anything we are waiting for or looking forward to in this life can and will disappoint, but we are also waiting for a certain end: victory in Christ. If our hope lies in Jesus, we trade the anxieties of an unknown world for the peace of a certain future. We can grab our tambourines. We can expect joy and goodness, even now, when the road ahead looks bleak.

And when all our plans are a shattered mess and everything we are looking forward to has been canceled or changed a million times, one thing can never be canceled: the love of God over you, over me, over us. That love of God that is promised, that is certain, that is always bringing us home to Him.

> For I am convinced that neither death nor life, neither angels nor demons, neither the present nor the future, nor any powers, neither height nor depth, nor anything else in all creation, will be able to separate us from the love of God that is in Christ Jesus our Lord.[9]

If we hope in anything other than Jesus and eternity, we *will* be disappointed. But when we stake our hope certainly on the promises of God, we can be sure that our hope is not in vain.

I THINK OF my little two-and-a-half-year-old screaming, "This is not my hooooooooome! Home, home, hooooooome. This is not my home!" This was his anthem for months after we moved, every time I told him we were going "home" from the store or the park or his sisters' school and then took him back to the newest unfamiliar residence.

"I know, buddy," I'd say. "I know this isn't home, but it's our home for now." Sometimes, often, I wanted to burst into tears with him.

This wasn't our home, and would we ever find home again? Would this new place ever feel like home, or would we one day go back to the home we so dearly loved and missed? Would I always feel like my heart was in two places, deeply grateful to be on the same continent as the rest of our family again while deeply missing the comforts and community of the place we had made our home?

I would think often of what C. S. Lewis wrote in *Mere Christianity:* "If I find in myself a desire which no experience in this world can satisfy, the most probable explanation is that I was made for another world."[10]

Maybe we truly would never feel completely at home again, and maybe this is evidence, our constant reminder that this world wasn't meant to be our permanent home because we were created for an-

## HOPE THAT WILL NOT DISAPPOINT

What are you looking forward to? What hope perches in your heart as you consider your present circumstances? Whatever it may be, how does the certainty of your promised home in heaven compare with that earthly hope?

How can you practice meditating on heaven more in your everyday life?

How can you shift your daily interactions with others, your daily tasks, even your daily thoughts and worries to reflect what you believe about heaven? How does the promise of good things up ahead free you to let go of your present anxiety and fear?

I invite you to read the following passage and identify some of the promises that speak hope to your heart. Write them down.

other. And as you and I take this journey into peace, as we repeatedly circle back to these same lessons—of trust and surrender and holding fast to the truth—and back to these same practices—of Bible study and prayer, remembrance, lament and worship, presence and discernment and rest, reconciliation and service—we will make our home *in* Him as we look forward to our eternal home *with* Him. The current in the river may change, but our God doesn't.

*Our deep, abiding peace will come from resting in the promised hope of heaven.*

Any peace we get from "knowing" our plans, from trying to control the future, is false and temporary. But a peace that comes from trusting in the certain promises of God will carry us along, bring us through, lead us home. The peace that comes from trusting in our

---

Meditate on them, especially when the troubles of the day feel overwhelming.

Then I saw "a new heaven and a new earth," for the first heaven and the first earth had passed away, and there was no longer any sea. I saw the Holy City, the new Jerusalem, coming down out of heaven from God, prepared as a bride beautifully dressed for her husband. And I heard a loud voice from the throne saying, "Look! God's dwelling place is now among the people, and he will dwell with them. They will be his people, and God himself will be with them and be their God. 'He will wipe every tear from their eyes. There will be no more death' or mourning or crying or pain, for the old order of things has passed away."

He who was seated on the throne said, "I am making everything new!"[19]

certain Father, who adores us, can never be canceled, can never lead us astray. "He who promised is faithful."[11]

When I moved to Uganda in 2007, not knowing the path, not knowing what God had in store for my life, truly not anxious about anything and resting in a deep certainty that He was going to take care of me, I named my blog "On Earth as It Is in Heaven." I truly believed that as I followed God into the unknown, He would make this true of my life. I had no idea then that I would make my home in Uganda for fifteen years, that I would build my career, meet my dearest friends, marry my husband, adopt and birth my children there. I had no idea what I would walk through, how I would doubt and rail against the dark and how God would meet me there.

"On earth as it is in heaven." I am not sure what I thought it meant exactly, but it sure sounded beautiful. Of course, it is a phrase plucked out of Jesus's prayer that He uses as an example for the disciples. "This, then, is how you should pray," He instructs. "Our Father in heaven, hallowed be your name, your kingdom come, your will be done, on earth as it is in heaven."[12] Maybe I thought that if we loved our neighbors hard enough, we'd somehow love our way out of the suffering. But we all know it: There is no love without pain, no path to perfect peace that doesn't lead us deep into the heart of hardship. While I do think Jesus is challenging us to obey Him and love each other as He prays this way, our love is never really enough to bind up the hurts of the world or even our own broken hearts. But His is, and He holds us. *He holds us now on earth as He will in heaven.*

Maybe that's the secret to the peace I long for. I can live here held—as I have always been, as I will always be—safe in His loving arms.

We are made for heaven, for this holding, whether or not we choose to acknowledge it. We are held, we are seen, we are known, we are beloved, just as we have always been, just as we will be in heaven.

Nothing gives me peace like imagining heaven, where we will forever be with Jesus, where the pains and inconveniences of this world will fade away. The more I make eternity the goal of my day, the less my thoughts spiral on other things. Truly, all the thoughts and distractions that come against my peace and steadiness feel so small in light of eternity. We look forward to that restored "Eden peace," knowing that it is ours in Christ. We know that one day we will truly be far above the rapids, able to see how He kept us, how He ordained all our steps, all our trials and all our joys, even the parts that didn't make any sense. How it was all for our good. How He never failed us. How we were safe all along.

God's dwelling place will be "among the people, and he will dwell with them. They will be his people, and God himself will be with them and be their God. He will wipe every tear from their eyes. There will be no more death or mourning or crying or pain."[13] Our story ends the same way it began: A faithful God chooses us, calls us beloved. When we find our home in Him, we find our deep peace, the peace He has always longed to lavish on us, on earth, as it will be in heaven.

ABOUT A YEAR after our move, on a quick spring-break trip to the beach, I stand at the edge of the ocean and watch the waves rhythmically lap at the shore. *Is it possible that we have been here almost a year?* Our other home in Uganda feels like yesterday and a lifetime ago. As the waves roll, I keep thinking of the four hundred years of silence between the last prophet of the Old Testament and the birth of Jesus, the Messiah. All those years of quiet and God was still moving, still working, still orchestrating His perfect redemption story. He was still intending to bring about the rescue of His beloved people through His precious Son. I wonder what it must have been like to live in that season of silence. How God's people remained faithful and waited in anticipation all those years. How men like Simeon continued to look forward to the Messiah even with no outward indication that He would soon appear. No indication *except the promises of God*. Luke says that Simeon "was eagerly waiting for the Messiah to come and rescue Israel."[14]

Four hundred years of silence, but even in the waiting, it is God's desire to reveal Himself to His people. He gives His star as a sign to the magi, then appears to them in a dream. He appears to Mary through an angel. He protects His Son and thus His people and His plan to redeem us. Whether through dreams or angels or—so much more often—through other people or the quiet whispers of the Spirit within us, His desire is to reveal Himself to us here while we wait.

And remember that promise Jesus made right before He went to the cross? "Peace I leave with you; my peace I give you."[15] Through His promised Holy Spirit, we can have this peace and wholeness right here, right now. He loved us enough to die. Certainly, He loves us enough to give us everything we need here and now too. As the psalmist assures us,

[God] crowns you with love and compassion. . . .

As high as the heavens are above the earth,
    so great is his love for those who fear him;
as far as the east is from the west,
    so far has he removed our transgressions from us.[16]

*He has already done everything needed to secure our perfect peace, our eternity with Him.* Because of His death on the cross and His glorious resurrection three days later, there will be a day when the whole earth, ourselves included, is made perfectly whole with no more sadness or suffering or fear or anxiety.

Here's the thing: If there hadn't been a cross and a tomb, there couldn't have been a resurrection. And so often to have a front-row seat to redemption, we have to dive headfirst into the hard, into the dark. And through it all, we can wait in hope because we trust in God.

Once we begin truly letting go of control, surrendering our plans, practicing presence and peace in the good seasons and the hard seasons and the middle seasons, we begin to realize that there is room for something we haven't had in a while: hope. There is room to dream, room to imagine, room to anticipate.

*What are you looking forward to?*

I LAY IN bed one night in our rented farmhouse and said to Benji, "It's not everything we imagined and we don't have everything figured out yet, but for the first time in a long time, I feel like I am able to see possibility."

In Jesus, there is always possibility.[17]

We can wait in anticipation for good things up ahead, even when we do not know what is in store.

In Isaiah 46:10–11, God declares that He "make[s] known the end from the beginning." He says, "My purpose will stand. . . . What I have said, that I will bring about; what I have planned, that I will do." I've been thinking about this verse a lot lately, especially as we have passed through several seasons of uncertainty.

There is a reason Paul and the writer of Hebrews repeatedly refer to life as a race, a journey requiring perseverance, strength, and, above all, the help of the Spirit.[18] The race is long, but when we dedicate our next steps, our choices, our decisions, our very lives to the Lord, He will give us what we need. He will equip us for what is ahead, all the while holding the end in His loving hands.

A good friend prayed over me a few years ago, "Lord, help us remember that it ends with us with You." This stuck. I go back to these
words and whisper them to myself on hard days. *Lord, this all ends
with us with You.*

God's finished work in the garden was good, His finished work
on the cross was good, and His finished work in eternity is good. If
you are looking around and things don't seem good now, you can
rest assured that is because God is not yet finished.

The picture of the idyllic garden in Eden where God first places
man and woman is strikingly similar to Revelation 22, a passage I
often read when I need some grounding and peace. But in verse 2, a
phrase is added that makes my breath catch in my throat a little: "The
leaves of the tree are for the healing of the nations."

*He intends our healing.* Not just physically in our new bodies but
spiritually, emotionally, holistically. In the restored Eden, the eternal
garden, there will be no curse and there will be no night. All things,
including us, will be perfectly whole and complete, *eiréné.* God, who
formed us of dust and breathed life into us, so desires to be with us
that we will one day look upon His face forever. *His finished work will
be good far beyond what we can imagine, and we will experience the
most complete and perfect peace.*

Beloved, if you are still reading this, it's not the end yet.

*God isn't finished yet.*

I think of Paul waiting for two years in prison, having already
received the promise that he would testify about Christ in Rome.
Were there days when he wondered how in the world he would get
there? I think of Abraham, insistent that God will bring Isaac a
spouse from his own country and family when that seemed utterly
impossible. I think of myself in my own seasons of uncertainty, when
I cannot yet see what God might be trying to accomplish, when it
doesn't quite appear that His plans *are,* in fact, good.

I can sit in my own "middle" places and look at my little tribe, feeling at a loss, overwhelmed, unequipped. But God knows the end from the beginning. And if this is the place He has called me, if these are the people He has given me, if this is the thing He has put in front of me, He *will* equip me for the next step, the next right choice.

Paul can tell the truth because he knows where it will end for him. Abraham can trust that God will fulfill His promise to make him a great nation, because he knows where it will end for him.

And we can stand firm, we can hope, we can believe, because we know what awaits us. We know that this is not all there is.

*His love is always coming for us.*

For us who are lost.

For us who are broken.

For us who have tried and failed and tried again.

For us who aren't sure where home even is right now.

There is nothing that we can't hope for, because nothing is impossible for the God whom the wind and the waves obey.

*Father, thank You that You are a God who makes promises to His people. Thank You that You are a God who keeps His promises. We confess that so often our current situation or circumstances do not seem light and momentary and we let our disappointment become all-consuming. Help us turn our gazes to You, to Your eternal glory. Thank You for the promise of eternity with You that we have to look forward to. Father, cause every other distraction and hardship to fall away in light of Your glorious promises. Help us look forward to spending forever with You. Amen.*

# EPILOGUE

## *Secure in His Hand*

You make known to me the path of life;
you will fill me with joy in your presence,
with eternal pleasures at your right hand.

—PSALM 16:11

"Come on! Come on!" our five-year-old son calls out to his little brother from the middle of the biggest puddle in our yard. Our littlest is standing at the edge, soaked by the rain but uncertain if he wants to venture into the puddle.

"Hey, it's really deep here. Grab my hand!" Big brother makes his way toward the end of the puddle and reaches out for his little brother. Trusting, little brother grabs on and follows his daring brother into the puddle that almost reaches his waist in the deepest part. I watch them walk away from me, hand in hand, and all I can think of is Jesus's hand reaching out to me in the midst of the waves.

*We need to be rescued.* We need to hear a voice saying, *It's deep here, love. Grab My hand.* In the deepest waves, in the darkest night, in the hardest season, our God reaches out His hand to us. And He doesn't let go. *He gives us His unshakable peace.*

He didn't let go of Joseph as he endured slavery and then prison. He didn't let Joseph stop believing in Him, hoping in Him, and no trial could thwart His good plan for Joseph.

He didn't let go of Israel, though they were fickle, worshipping one day and blaspheming the next, defiling the temple, and appearing full of fruit though they were not. He died for them anyway, longing, always longing, to draw them to Himself.

He didn't let go of David, though the world was against him, though he would hide in caves and run for his life from his own son, though he cried out in anguish and flooded his bed with weeping. The Lord heard his cry and used his life and gave him the strength to worship, regardless of his doubt or despair.

He didn't let go of Hagar when she couldn't see what was right in front of her, when her doubt and despair blinded her, but graciously opened her eyes to life-giving water.

He didn't let go of me when things looked and felt impossible, and He won't let go of you, dear one.

"Anyone who believes in him will never be put to shame."[1]

~

I'VE BEEN BACK to the Nile River a few times since that first experience, but it was only after several visits that I was able to spend time there without my stomach churning with worry or my mind racing with what-ifs. And when I got brave enough to paddle my board out of the bay and into the open river, I asked Benji only once if he really thought I could make it back.

"Of course you can," he replied, and when Benji and I did successfully paddle across and back again, I heard myself whisper, "We are stronger than we thought."

It has been several years since I first felt like my entire life was being turned upside down, since I thought all my worst and hardest "life rapids" were over and conquered, only to be pummeled again and again. A river just keeps moving and life just keeps coming.

And we are stronger than we think. We are stronger than we think because *God is holding us more securely than we know.* He doesn't let go even when we don't feel Him, and His good purposes for us don't change even as we are pummeled by the waves or paddling hard against the current. Every day, we are learning to surrender; we are learning to trust; we are learning peace.

Benji and I spent that day on the river, and miraculously I didn't worry much about our future, even though we were in Uganda for only three weeks and then headed back to the United States for an undefined amount of time. Sure, my mind wanted to race ahead and make some plans. I imagine I will always be wired that way. But mostly I just couldn't get over the beauty of the sun shining off the water and the flowers blooming on the bank, the indistinct chatter of people far off and the rush of the river in my ears. I watched a brilliantly clad kingfisher and remembered these words of Jesus in the book of Matthew:

> Look at the birds. They don't plant or harvest or store food in barns, for your heavenly Father feeds them. And aren't you far more valuable to him than they are? . . .
>
> Look at the lilies of the field and how they grow. They don't work or make their clothing, yet Solomon in all his glory was not dressed as beautifully as they are. And if God cares so wonderfully for wildflowers that are here today and thrown into the fire tomorrow, he will certainly care for you.[2]

He has certainly cared for us. He certainly does care for us. He will certainly care for us. Herein lies our peace.

I breathed deep that humid, tropical air and the grace of just being here, right now. Steady. *Or at least a little steadier than yesterday.* Less confident in my own ability to control and plot and plan, more certain than ever of God's trustworthy love and sovereignty. Learning to live in the unshakable peace that comes from knowing Him, from His love drawing us deeper and deeper in. The waves tried to take us out, but God held us. I couldn't see what was up ahead, around the corner, but He knew.

And the waves, all the struggles? They make us better somehow. They've made me softer in the places that used to be calloused, filled with greater understanding and empathy, more flexible and less controlling, more accepting and less judgmental, less sure I know anything and more sure that I have so much to learn.

I'm willing to bet that you, too, feel a bit beaten and bruised from the rapids of this life. I think you'll agree that there's probably no way to avoid them entirely. But God, who *does* see what is up ahead, is using all of it to make us who He intends for us to be. I am a fuller, better version of myself because of the rapids God has allowed, and I can testify that He has carried me and formed me and shaped me through all of them. Might you be ready today to join your testimony with mine, to declare that He has been with you in the deep waters and the flames of life?[3]

He always sees the view from above. Until He calls you home to Himself, He's always providing a way; He is always seeing the whole plan; He is always intending our rescue. Jesus isn't surprised by our easily distracted nature, our outright rebellion, or our identity crises. He knew the Israelites, remember? He knows our frame. And He also knows all that the world is going to throw against us, all the waves we are up against, the storms we will weather. He promises that He gives us peace right in the middle of it all. In Philippians 3, Paul said,

Not that I have already obtained all this, or have already arrived at my goal, but I press on to take hold of that for which

Christ Jesus took hold of me. Brothers and sisters, I do not
consider myself yet to have taken hold of it. But one thing I do:
Forgetting what is behind and straining toward what is ahead,
I press on toward the goal to win the prize for which God has
called me heavenward in Christ Jesus.[4]

We press on. We press on toward the prize—eternity with our
loving Father who Himself is our deep and abiding peace. Isaiah 26:3
says, "You will keep in perfect peace those whose minds are steadfast, because they trust in you." We trust. We hope. We surrender. We
leave our guilt and our anxiety and our control at His feet and move
toward greater trust, toward a Father who is waiting with His arms
outstretched, toward eternity with Him. Eyes on Jesus, our perfect
Peace.

"YOU DID IT, buddy! We did it!" The boys finally make it across the
puddle. They look back to be sure that I've seen, my little ones looking for me, making sure I am still there, making sure they are still
safe.

And I exhale, deeply assured that I am beloved of a strong and
kind, safe and merciful God and that when I cannot see anything
else, I can fix my gaze on Him.

If you are in the middle of your deepest pain, I pray you know
Him there in the boat with you. If you feel that the rapids of doubt
and confusion and anxiety might just pull you under, I pray you
know that He is never going to let you drown. If you are in a season
of great contentment and joy, I pray you exhale thanks to the God
who brought you here and walks beside you. And if you, like I am,
are right in the messy middle, still trying to figure it all out, where

the joy and the sad and the good and the uncertain and the down-right awful are all tangled up together, I pray that you experience the deep peace that comes from knowing that God sees the whole path, the whole river, and has intentions only to bring you safely home. The deep peace that is found only in Jesus.

In Him, we are safe all along.

# VERSES TO REMIND YOU OF THE GOD WHO HOLDS YOU SAFE

You will keep in perfect peace those whose minds are steadfast, because they trust in you. (Isaiah 26:3)

I have seen you in the sanctuary and beheld your power and your glory. Because your love is better than life, my lips will glorify you. (Psalm 63:2–3)

Peace I leave with you; my peace I give you. I do not give you as the world gives. Do not let your hearts be troubled and do not be afraid. (John 14:27)

Do not be anxious about anything, but in every situation, by prayer and petition, with thanksgiving, present your requests to God. And the peace of God, which transcends all understanding, will guard your hearts and your minds in Christ Jesus. (Philippians 4:6–7)

Do not fear, for I have redeemed you; I have summoned you by name; you are mine. When you pass through the waters, I will be with you; and when you pass through the rivers, they will not sweep over you. (Isaiah 43:1–2)

The wisdom that comes from heaven is first of all pure; then peace-loving, considerate, submissive, full of mercy and good fruit, impartial and sincere. Peacemakers who sow in peace reap a harvest of righteousness. (James 3:17–18)

Trust in the LORD with all your heart and lean not on your own understanding; in all your ways submit to him, and he will make your paths straight. (Proverbs 3:5–6)

We know that in all things God works for the good of those who love him, who have been called according to his purpose. (Romans 8:28)

My flesh and my heart may fail, but God is the strength of my heart and my portion forever. (Psalm 73:26)

God has not given us a spirit of fear, but of power and of love and of a sound mind. (2 Timothy 1:7, NKJV)

Cast all your anxiety on him because he cares for you. (1 Peter 5:7)

"Though the mountains be shaken and the hills be removed, yet my unfailing love for you will not be shaken nor my covenant of peace be removed," says the LORD, who has compassion on you. (Isaiah 54:10)

I am convinced that neither death nor life, neither angels nor demons, neither the present nor the future, nor any powers, neither height nor depth, nor anything else in all creation, will be able to separate us from the love of God that is in Christ Jesus our Lord. (Romans 8:38–39)

He brought me out into a spacious place; he rescued me because he delighted in me. (Psalm 18:19)

The LORD your God is with you, the Mighty Warrior who saves. He will take great delight in you; in his love he will no longer rebuke you, but will rejoice over you with singing. (Zephaniah 3:17)

You will go out in joy and be led forth in peace. (Isaiah 55:12)

Let us hold unswervingly to the hope we profess, for he who
  promised is faithful. (Hebrews 10:23)
They will see his face, and his name will be on their foreheads.
  There will be no more night. They will not need the light of a
  lamp or the light of the sun, for the Lord God will give them
  light. And they will reign for ever and ever. (Revelation 22:4–5)

# ACKNOWLEDGMENTS

Truly, to pull off a project like this book requires the love, support, and prayers of almost every person in my life, and it seems impossible to express my deep gratitude to each one. This has been not just a writing journey but a life journey, a healing journey, that isn't possible without an entire community of people who walked it with me.

To my family, who make sacrifices in order to allow me to do this work, to share glimpses of our lives with the world, who endure a messier-than-usual house or a little too much takeout. You are the joy of my life. That God gave me each one of you to walk through life with me astounds me—it is my greatest privilege. I am in constant awe of the way you have weathered the waves and continued loving Jesus, me, and one another. Thank you. *I love you forever.*

Karen and Curtis and the rest of the team at Yates & Yates, thank you for being my friends, for believing in me long before the rest of the world did. Thank you for time and time again helping make my dreams reality.

Laura, I still cannot believe I get to work with someone as Spirit-filled and talented as you. Thank you for making me a better writer, for living this message, for loving Jesus more than anything. I can't imagine doing this without you, and I am thankful I don't have to. You live as a person of the Father's unshakable peace, and I am grateful not just for your editing but for your example.

To the entire Multnomah team, this many years later I am still giddy that I get to work with such an amazing team of people who love the Lord. Thank you for believing in me and the words that He lays on my heart. Thank you for praying and cheering and loving Jesus with your lives. I am so grateful.

To our people—the ones in Tennessee and the ones in Uganda, the ones we have known forever and the ones who became our instant family when we found ourselves so far from home. My eyes fill with grateful tears when I think of the way you have all shown up for us. You drove through the traffic and you sat on our couches and you loved our children. You sent the texts and made the calls and prayed in hope when I couldn't muster hope for myself. You came around us as the beautiful body of Christ that you are, up close and from a distance. Your stories, our conversations, and your encouragements are woven into the book because you pointed me always to Jesus. I'll never get over the gift of you.

I sit here at the end of this book, this season, this learning and growing, with the deepest gratitude to my Father God, who loved me, who rescued me, who held on to me when I could not hold on to Him, who is always drawing me deeper. Lord, all I have is Yours, and You are all I desire. Draw me deeper still.

# NOTES

CHAPTER ONE: THE VIEW FROM ABOVE

1. Yes, "up the river." Fun fact: The Nile River runs south to north.
2. See Romans 8:28.
3. Psalm 73:26.
4. Isaiah 43:1–3.
5. John 14:27.

CHAPTER TWO: PULLED APART

1. 2 Timothy 1:7, NKJV.
2. Philippians 4:6.
3. Colossians 3:15.
4. Matthew 6:25.
5. 1 Peter 5:7.
6. *Strong's Concordance* 3307, s.v. "*merimna,*" https://biblehub.com/greek/3307.htm; 3308, https://biblehub.com/greek/3308.htm; 3309, https://biblehub.com/greek/3309.htm. The verb form is *merimnaó.*
7. See Mark 6:7–12.
8. See Mark 6:14–29.
9. See Mark 6:30–44.
10. See Mark 6:48.

11. Mark 6:50.
12. See 2 Timothy 1:7, NKJV.

CHAPTER THREE: AS IT WAS IN THE BEGINNING

1. Genesis 1:1–2.
2. Genesis 1:2.
3. Genesis 1:3.
4. Genesis 3:1.
5. See Genesis 3:2–3.
6. See Genesis 3:4.
7. See Genesis 3:5.
8. See Numbers 11.
9. See Acts 7:52–53.
10. See Genesis 3:6–8.
11. See Genesis 3:9–13.
12. Isaiah 54:10.

CHAPTER FOUR: THE SEARCH FOR SHALOM

1. See Ephesians 2:14.
2. John 14:27.
3. John 16:33.
4. John 16:7.
5. Matthew 28:20.
6. Luke 7:50; 8:48.
7. *Strong's Concordance* 1515, s.v. *"eiréné,"* https://biblehub.com/greek/1515.htm.
8. Isaiah 43:2–3.
9. Isaiah 43:4, ESV.
10. Isaiah 43:1, ESV.
11. John 14:27.
12. See Philippians 4:7.
13. See Romans 8:38–39.

CHAPTER FIVE: CONTROL FREAK

1. See Genesis 27.
2. Genesis 32:7, 9–11.
3. See Genesis 32:7–8, 13–15.
4. See Genesis 32:24–26.
5. Genesis 32:27–31.
6. Genesis 33:1, 3–5, ESV.

7. Genesis 33:10.
8. Romans 7:15.

CHAPTER SIX: TRUSTING THE FATHER'S TENDER LOVE

1. Luke 15:12.
2. Luke 15:17–19.
3. Psalm 38:4.
4. See Romans 7:15.
5. Luke 15:20.
6. Luke 15:20, ESV.
7. See Romans 2:4.
8. Luke 15:21–24, ESV.
9. Matthew 6:25–30.
10. Matthew 6:33, ESV.
11. See John 14:1.
12. See Genesis 3:21.
13. See Hebrews 12:2.
14. See Mark 6:51.
15. Matthew 14:28.
16. See Matthew 14:29–30.
17. See Matthew 14:31.
18. See Mark 9:24.

CHAPTER SEVEN: OUR STORYTELLING GOD

1. Mark 9:24.
2. See Romans 8:29.
3. See Psalm 18:19; Zephaniah 3:17.
4. Romans 8:1, 28, 31–33, 35, 37.
5. Curt Thompson, "Bringing Beauty to Chaos," presentation, IF:Gathering, Dallas, March 5, 2022.
6. See Isaiah 61:10.
7. Acts 9:4.
8. Acts 9:5.
9. See Galatians 1:11–12.
10. 1 Timothy 1:16.
11. See Psalm 103:8; Titus 3:4–6.
12. See Psalm 118:6; Romans 8:31.
13. See Romans 8:28; 1 Corinthians 2:9.
14. See Ephesians 1:11; Colossians 1:16–17.
15. See Romans 5:8; 1 John 3:1.

16.  See Genesis 1:27; Colossians 3:10.
17.  See John 15:16; Romans 8:29–30; Ephesians 1:5; 1 Peter 2:9.
18.  See Isaiah 43:7; Ephesians 2:10.
19.  See 1 Corinthians 15:57; Philippians 4:12–13; 1 John 5:4.

CHAPTER EIGHT: PRACTICE MAKES PROGRESS

1.  Judges 6:13.
2.  Judges 6:16.
3.  Matthew 8:25, ESV.
4.  Matthew 8:26.
5.  See Psalm 103:14, ESV.
6.  Mark 4:39, ESV.
7.  Isaiah 26:3.
8.  Judges 6:23–24.
9.  Philippians 4:6.
10.  Philippians 4:7.

CHAPTER NINE: KNOWING HIM

1.  See Matthew 4:1.
2.  Matthew 4:4, 7, 10.
3.  Matthew 4:4; see Deuteronomy 8:3.
4.  John 15:4, 5.
5.  See Isaiah 55:9.
6.  Hebrews 4:12.
7.  Ephesians 1:4, ESV.
8.  J. I. Packer, *Concise Theology: A Guide to Historic Christian Beliefs* (Wheaton, Ill.: Tyndale, 1993), 3.
9.  See Exodus 32:16.
10.  See 2 Peter 1:20–21.
11.  Galatians 6:9.
12.  Psalm 91:2–4.
13.  See Ephesians 2:14.
14.  John 15:4.
15.  See Acts 4:13.
16.  Psalm 19:7–10.

CHAPTER TEN: OUR CLOSEST FRIEND

1.  Psalm 139:1–4, ESV.
2.  See James 4:8.
3.  Philippians 4:6, NKJV.

4. See Mark 6:45–46.
5. See Isaiah 55.
6. Genesis 32:30.
7. See 1 John 3:1.
8. See John 15:15.
9. See 2 Corinthians 5:17.
10. See Psalm 103:4.
11. See Psalm 103:8–10.
12. Psalm 54:4.
13. Isaiah 40:28, esv.
14. Psalm 145:8.

CHAPTER ELEVEN: STONES AND BREAD

1. See Numbers 11:4–35.
2. Psalm 77:11–12.
3. Genesis 28:16–17.
4. See Genesis 35:1–15.
5. Deuteronomy 4:21.
6. Deuteronomy 1:29–31.
7. Deuteronomy 29:5.
8. Joshua 4:21–24, esv.
9. 1 Samuel 7:12.
10. Psalm 78:4, esv.
11. Psalm 78:7, esv.
12. 1 Corinthians 11:23–26.
13. Matthew 26:26.
14. See 1 Corinthians 11:25–26.

CHAPTER TWELVE: COME AS YOU ARE

1. 1 Samuel 7:12.
2. Psalm 13:1–2, 5–6.
3. Isaiah 61:1.
4. Job 1:8.
5. See Job 38:4.
6. See Job 38:12.
7. See Job 38:22, 24.
8. See Job 38:27.
9. 1 Samuel 13:14.
10. Psalm 6:2–4.
11. Luke 22:42.

12. See Hebrews 12:2.
13. 2 Corinthians 4:8–9.
14. See Psalm 31.
15. Morgan Harper Nichols, *Peace Is a Practice: An Invitation to Breathe Deep and Find a New Rhythm for Life* (Grand Rapids, Mich.: Zondervan, 2022), 39.
16. Matthew 27:46.
17. Psalm 34:18.
18. See 1 John 4:8.
19. See Exodus 34:6.
20. See Hebrews 13:8.
21. See Psalm 145:17.
22. See Hebrews 10:23.

CHAPTER THIRTEEN: WORSHIP ALONG THE WAY

1. Psalm 13:1–2, 5–6.
2. John Piper (@JohnPiper), "Occasionally weep deeply over the life you hoped would be. Grieve the losses. Then wash your face. Trust God. And embrace the life you have," Twitter, March 1, 2016, 6:04 A.M., https://twitter.com/johnpiper/status/704653441533132800?lang=en.
3. Laurie Klein, "I Love You, Lord" (House of Mercy Music, 1978).
4. See Psalm 30:11.
5. Acts 16:26.
6. See Acts 16:31–34.
7. Lamentations 3:21–23.
8. Lamentations 3:24–26.
9. Lamentations 3:1–2, 11, 19.
10. Lamentations 3:21.
11. Helen Keller, *The Open Door* (New York: Doubleday, 1957), 51.
12. Isaiah 55:12.
13. See Genesis 21:15–19.
14. Genesis 16:13.
15. Philippians 4:4.
16. Philippians 4:5–6.
17. See Philippians 4:5–7.
18. Psalm 126:2–3, 5.
19. See Exodus 15:1–21.
20. Exodus 15:2, ESV.

CHAPTER FOURTEEN: DWELL IN THE LAND

1. Psalm 91:1–2.
2. Matthew 6:28, ESV.
3. Psalm 37:3.
4. Psalm 37:4, ESV.
5. Psalm 91:1–2.
6. Jim Elliot as quoted in Elisabeth Elliot, *Through Gates of Splendor* (Wheaton, Ill.: Tyndale, 1983), 20.
7. Morgan Harper Nichols, *Peace Is a Practice: An Invitation to Breathe Deep and Find a New Rhythm for Life* (Grand Rapids, Mich.: Zondervan, 2022), 52.

CHAPTER FIFTEEN: THE BETTER THING

1. Matthew 10:16, ESV.
2. John 1:6–7, 19–20, ESV.
3. See Luke 1:41.
4. John 1:23, ESV.
5. John 1:29, 34, ESV.
6. See Philippians 1:9–11.
7. Colossians 1:9–10.
8. Luke 10:41–42.
9. See Exodus 31:13.

CHAPTER SIXTEEN: THE MINISTRY OF RECONCILIATION

1. Romans 3:23.
2. See Romans 7:15.
3. Sally Lloyd-Jones, *The Jesus Storybook Bible: Every Story Whispers His Name* (Grand Rapids, Mich.: Zonderkidz, 2007), 276.
4. Leviticus 26:3–4, 6, 11–12.
5. See Judges 6.
6. 2 Corinthians 5:18–21, ESV.
7. Philippians 2:6–8.
8. Genesis 33:10.
9. Genesis 50:20–21, ESV.
10. Romans 12:18.
11. Psalm 139:23–24, NKJV.

CHAPTER SEVENTEEN: A TOWEL AND A BASIN

1. 1 Thessalonians 2:8.
2. Galatians 5:13.

3. John 13:4–5, 12–15.
4. See Matthew 22:37–39.
5. Philippians 2:3–4.

CHAPTER EIGHTEEN: AN ETERNAL GLORY

1. See Genesis 21:5.
2. See Genesis 37:1–11.
3. Genesis 39:2.
4. See Genesis 39:21.
5. 2 Corinthians 4:16–18.
6. See Genesis 40:8.
7. Genesis 50:24, ESV.
8. See Isaiah 25:8.
9. Romans 8:38–39.
10. C. S. Lewis, *Mere Christianity,* rev. ed. (New York: HarperCollins, 2001), 136–37.
11. Hebrews 10:23.
12. Matthew 6:9–10.
13. Revelation 21:3–4.
14. Luke 2:25, NLT.
15. John 14:27.
16. Psalm 103:4, 11–12.
17. See Matthew 19:26.
18. See Acts 20:24; 1 Corinthians 9:24; 2 Timothy 4:7; Hebrews 12:1–3.
19. Revelation 21:1–5.

EPILOGUE: SECURE IN HIS HAND

1. Romans 10:11.
2. Matthew 6:26, 28–30, NLT.
3. See Isaiah 43:2.
4. Philippians 3:12–14.

*An invitation to cling to the God of the impossible*
*—in every circumstance and situation.*

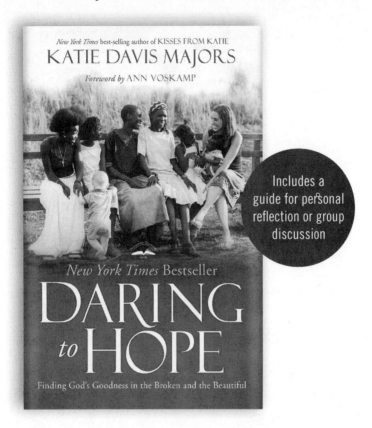

Includes a guide for personal reflection or group discussion

In *Daring to Hope*, Katie shares her ongoing experiences in Uganda as a wife, mother, and friend. This powerful, spiritually honest memoir describes how she wrestles through the darkness of disappointment to find a hope that does not disappoint.

**MULTNOMAH**

WaterBrookMultnomah.com

# AMAZIMA
## MINISTRIES

Founded by Katie Davis Majors in 2008 and fueled by a desire to see lives, communities, and relationships transformed by the hope of Jesus, Amazima's mission is to make disciples through **authentic relationships**, **excellent education**, and **strengthened communities**.

LEARN MORE ABOUT PARTNERING WITH AMAZIMA TO RAISE UP LEADERS AND IMPACT GENERATIONS IN UGANDA.
**amazima.org/hope**

 @AMAZIMA     @AMAZIMA     @AMAZIMA     AMAZIMA MINISTRIES